Sovereignty

Concepts in Social Thought

Series Editor: Frank Parkin

Published Titles

Concepts in Social Thought

Sovereignty

John Hoffman

University of Minnesota Press
Minneapolis

First published by Open University Press 1998

Published simultaneously in the United States 1998
by the University of Minnesota Press
111 Third Avenue South, Suite 290, Minneapolis, MN 55401-2520
http://www.upress.umn.edu

Printed in Great Britain

Library of Congress Cataloging-in-Publication Data
Hoffman, John, 1944–
    Sovereignty/John Hoffman.
      p.   cm. – (Concepts in social thought)
    Published simultaneously by: Open University Press, 1998.
    Includes bibliographical references and index.
    ISBN 0-8166-3303-7 (alk. paper). – ISBN 0-8166-3304-5 (pbk.
  alk. paper)
    1. Sovereignty.   I. Title.   II.Series.
JC327.H64   1998
320.1'5—dc21   98-17005
                                          CIP

ISBN 0-8166-3303-7 (hc)
ISBN 0-8166-3304-5 (pb)

The University of Minnesota is an equal-opportunity educator and
employer.

*To the memory of Jubalani Nobleman Nxumalo
('Comrade Mzala') who would have liked bits
of this book but disapproved of others*

Contents

Acknowledgements

I am grateful to the University of Leicester for granting me a sabbatical which made it possible to write this book. John Young, as Head of the Department of Politics, has been very supportive, and Robert Garner shouldered added administrative burdens which arose as a result of my absence.

Mike Levin took time from a busy schedule to comment upon a draft of the book. So did Laura Brace and Keith Faulks. I am indebted to all of them for advice and criticisms. Gillian Youngs looked at the chapter on realism and her response was invaluable. Thanks are also due to Ian Harris who provided useful bibliographical help, while Keith Willis supplied me with all the references to sovereignty in Simone de Beauvoir's *The Second Sex*.

While I was completing this book, a volume of articles which I edited with Laura Brace was published, and I am grateful to Petra Rechter of Cassell for permission to draw upon my article, 'Is It Time to Detach Sovereignty from the State?', which appears in that volume.

Special thanks to Rowan, Fred and Frieda for putting up with my preoccupation with what they doubtless regarded as an obscure and esoteric subject.

1
Introduction

One of the most distinguished experts on international relations has described sovereignty as a 'bothersome' concept.[1] This is certainly true, but I hope to show that it is a concept worth bothering about. It bothers our politicians, it bothers the public and it bothers academics. It has long bothered me.

Like many academics, I regard conferences with other academics as a slice of real life from which all manner of lessons can be learnt. Some years ago I attended an international conference in which I found that my attempts to brush sovereignty aside as an incoherent concept were dismissed out of hand. It was a bruising experience. Objections to sovereignty were put down to a simplistic misunderstanding of a concept too well established to be so easily dismissed. Is not the reality of sovereignty self-evident? Article 2 of the United Nations Charter speaks of the sovereign equality of all its members, and, judging by the number of states which have been recognized as sovereign in international law in the past decade, sovereignty is becoming more popular than ever before.

My critics were right. Sovereignty cannot be dismissed out of hand, and in this book I argue that the concept should not (indeed cannot) be abandoned. At the same time, what makes it peculiarly bothersome is the disagreement which it provokes. So important is the contention which surrounds sovereignty that I have devoted the whole of Chapter 2 to the subject. Some have even argued that because sovereignty is so contentious, it cannot be defined. Sovereignty, they suggest, is intertwined with our notions of meaning and truth, so that trying to pin sovereignty down is like asking a religious person to define God. How do you pigeon-hole something which is the creator of all pigeon-holes?

Sovereignty is an insoluble problem – I agree with this point – but it is insoluble only as long as we associate it with the state. I have become convinced that this linkage takes us to the heart of the problem. A statist view of sovereignty has certainly been the source of my own difficulties. It is true that in the conference in 1992 (recalled above) I was critical of the state. But I took the view that sovereignty and the state went together: in criticizing the one, it was necessary to criticize the other. When I wrote *Beyond the State* soon afterwards,[2] I still saw sovereignty as indissolubly linked to the state. I now accept, as I shall argue in this book, that *the link between the two can and must be severed*, and that, when this is done, the concept of sovereignty can be reformulated and 'reclaimed'.[3]

In Chapter 2 I concede that, like all concepts in politics, sovereignty arouses controversy or contention. But I distinguish between the kind of contention which paralyses and the kind of contention which stimulates, arguing that sovereignty can only act as a stimulating concept when it is detached from the state. Adherents of the so-called 'realist' school of international relations have, as I note in Chapter 3, taken the link between sovereignty and the state for granted. Hence, when it comes to the question of contention, they have a problem. Any attempt to relate sovereignty to what they see as 'internal' political issues such as democracy, the rule of law, autonomy or freedom would plunge the concept into the very controversy which has led some to argue for its abandonment. Realists take the view that sovereignty *can* be freed from contention, but only when we confine ourselves to the analysis of sovereign states in international relations.

Alan James's book on sovereignty is an excellent example of the realist argument that sovereignty is best defined in formal terms.[4] James is acutely aware that in the international realm, states are influenced by other states and are unable to do as they please. Sovereignty cannot therefore mean something substantive such as autonomy, political independence or freedom from constraint. It is a legal term, he argues, which simply denotes constitutional independence. But this is a solution, I suggest in Chapter 3, which creates more problems than it solves. For what happens when the sovereignty of a particular state is challenged by other states which are not persuaded by its claims to constitutional independence? James, like all realists, has to fall back upon the argument that what counts at the end of the day is the effectiveness of the state. Institutions which can plausibly claim to exercise a monopoly of legitimate force are sovereign.

But this, I argue, plunges realism into the very contention it seeks to avoid. For what makes the state supremely contentious is the fact that it claims a monopoly of legitimate force which it does not and cannot possess. Realists can only keep contention at bay as long as the state itself seems unproblematic.

Modernity and legitimacy

The link between the state and sovereignty could be challenged by arguing that sovereignty is the product of modern states – not states in general. This is an important point because if the sovereign state is identified solely with modernity, then it follows that states in the pre-modern past were not sovereign, and there might be states in a postmodern future which are not sovereign. The need to look beyond the state itself is called into question.

In Chapter 4 I engage with the argument that sovereignty must be analysed in historical terms. I accept that states have changed over time and so has sovereignty. But this point can only be grasped if we argue that all states claim a monopoly of legitimate force (albeit in different ways), and that it is this claim to exercise a monopoly of force which makes states appear sovereign. The ancient Greeks had already commented on the *supreme* power of rulers, and so had medieval thinkers. It is true that in pre-modern texts the term 'sovereignty' is not yet used (indeed, the same point could be made about the state), but it does not follow that because the sovereign state is only explicitly identified in the modern period, it had no existence before then. The concept of sovereignty as it is articulated from the sixteenth century onwards by European thinkers, can only be understood if we note the way in which earlier and archaic concepts of state sovereignty were built upon and transformed.

I do not deny the importance of sovereignty analysed in modern terms. On the contrary, if we are to understand what is distinctive about the modernist concept, we need to adopt a broad view of state sovereignty. For modernism (or modernity) brings to a head problems latent in the notion of state sovereignty from the start. Modernists insist upon sovereignty as absolute and unrestrained power. At the same time, they argue that this power must be limited. It is this combination of *both* attributes – each of which receives equal emphasis – that makes the concept so paradoxical. Modernity is important to sovereignty, not because sovereignty is simply a modern idea, but because by arguing that it must be both absolute and limited, modernists enable us to see why sovereignty is an impossibly contentious concept when it is linked to the state.

In Chapter 5 I explore sovereignty in relation to legitimacy and force. Modernism focuses explicitly upon this question since it seeks to limit the power of the state through acknowledging the rights of the individual. Legitimacy arises from limits, but the problem is that if sovereignty is expressed through the state's claim to exercise a monopoly of legitimate force, how are these limits to be enforced?

'Legitimate force' is a contradiction in terms. The limits associated with the concept of legitimacy provide space for the individual to act freely, express choice and exercise consent. However, it is precisely this space which force consumes. Modernists recognize the collision between force and freedom, and yet consider that the force of the state is indispensable to attaining order. This assumption, most famously associated with Thomas Hobbes, has to be challenged, and I draw upon the evidence of post-war anthropology to show that people can, and for millions of years have, governed themselves without a state. They have, in other words, not relied upon force as a method of resolving conflicts of interest.

To understand how this is possible, we need to distinguish both between state and government and between force and coercion. Government simply involves resolving conflicts of interest; the state, on the other hand, seeks to do this through force. While I accept that coercion is inherent in all social relationships, in Chapter 5 I contend that coercion is not the same as force. People still retain a capacity to act, exercise choice and enjoy freedom when they are coerced, whereas this subjective identity is crushed when force is used. Force dehumanizes both victor and victim. Hence its continued usage in state-centred societies undermines legitimacy for everyone.

Democracy, feminism and postmodernism

Three arguments in particular challenge state sovereignty. I devote separate chapters to examining them in detail, since each provides material for constructing a concept of sovereignty which goes beyond the state.

The democratic argument has often been used to suggest that state sovereignty is irrelevant in the modern world. The problem with this argument, however, is that if democracy is defined as a self-governing *state*, then popular rule is deemed to express itself through hierarchical and repressive institutions. Federalist systems, for example, do not jettison the principle of state sovereignty so long as they disallow secession: as states, they too embrace institutions which claim a monopoly of legitimate force. The notion of the 'people' defined in a statist way is treacherously ideological. As the experience of democracy in the United States demonstrates, large numbers of people may be explicitly excluded from processes which are supposed to embrace all.

In Chapter 6 I also tackle the argument that democracy rests upon a notion of popular sovereignty which suppresses diversity and pluralism. The problem with this 'tyranny thesis', as I call it, is that it confuses democracy with the state, and fails to see that identifying politics with conciliatory methods of conflict resolution is only possible if we challenge the need for force. It is not democracy or indeed the concept of popular sovereignty which is the problem: it is the state.

This is why David Held's important work on cosmopolitan democracy runs into difficulty. He defines sovereignty as an authority which embraces transnational, regional and local associations: at the same time, he continues to identify sovereignty with the state.[5] As a result, both politics and the state are presented in contradictory ways. Politics is sometimes seen as state-centred; at other times it is a social process which seeks to strengthen the freedom and autonomy of individuals. At some points in his argument, the state is an institution which claims a monopoly of force; at others it is simply a national organization which administers and governs. This confusion leads Held to argue that a cosmopolitan democracy has to limit popular sovereignty. The most awkward 'others' need to be excluded from the *demos*, and freedom and autonomy are ideals which cannot, when all is said and done, actually come to fruition in the real world.

If democracy is one concept which seeks to challenge state sovereignty, feminism is another. But feminism has become so diverse that it is not clear whether it is possible to speak of a feminist position on sovereignty at all. In Chapter 7 I argue that feminism is best defined as a general critique of patriarchy. Feminism has an emancipatory 'logic' which is undermined when attempts are made to isolate as separate variants, arguments which contribute to the freedom and autonomy of women as a whole.

Feminism is an argument which challenges the hierarchical and patriarchal institutions of the state. It is true that some feminists dispute the need for a feminist theory of state sovereignty, but this reluctance to criticize the state arises, I argue, from a failure to distinguish between statism as an expression of force, and government as an activity which involves administration. It is only through questioning the state itself that it becomes possible to disentangle sovereignty as freedom and autonomy, from sovereignty as a divisive and hierarchical attribute of the state.

Kathleen Jones has argued persuasively for the notion of 'compassionate authority'.[6] At the same time, she refers to sovereignty as inherently patriarchal. But why can't the idea of sovereignty be reworked so that it denotes the capacity of women as 'others' to govern their own lives? Sovereignty does not have to involve domination and oppression. It can be 'feminized' to embrace the power of individuals to relate to others in ways which strengthen rather than undermine self-esteem and self-determination. This is why it is important to build upon the liberal tradition. On the one hand, liberalism stresses the rights of individuals to control their own lives. On the other hand, liberalism also accepts the necessity of the state, and it does so because it conceives of people as atomistic, property-owning individuals whose freedom rests upon the exclusion of others. The notion of 'self-sovereignty' which some feminist writers adopt, is an important one, but it needs to be interpreted in a way which challenges the repressive hierarchies inherent in the state.

If feminism and democracy represent conceptual challenges to state sovereignty, so too does postmodernism. I identify postmodernism with a subversive logic that rejects static ideas, hierarchical methods of thought and abstract concepts. Postmodernists focus in particular upon what they call 'logocentrism' – the presentation of conceptual categories in an exclusionary and divisive way so that if one 'side' is right, the other must be wrong. No space is allowed for compromise, ambiguity or toleration. In Chapter 7 I argue that logocentrism as a theoretical expression of modernity fits the practice of the state like a glove. For states only exist because the claim they make to exercise a monopoly of legitimate force is contested. They presuppose the presence of those whom they necessarily exclude.

But logocentrism is not only a problem for the state. It is also a problem for those who reject the state in an abstract and arbitrary manner. Postmodernism warns against adopting the 'heroic practice' of criticizing institutions in a way which fails to move beyond them. A 'utopian' rejection of the state is as empty as a 'realistic' endorsement of it, and many emancipatory bodies of thought offer fictional solutions to real problems by looking to an abstractly conceived actor or principle to provide an answer.

Challenging state sovereignty involves 'deconstruction' – a method of criticizing things from within – so that alternatives emerge from the real world itself. Not all postmodernists, however, utilize deconstruction in a consistently critical manner. Some retreat from the subversive logic of the position they ostensibly support by embracing a relativism which simply turns modernism inside out. Deconstruction, I argue, can only contribute meaningfully to the development of a post-statist concept of sovereignty if we recognize the centrality of modernist ideas and institutions. The modernist idea of an international society composed of sovereign states contains the seeds of its own conceptual subversion, since once we acknowledge that all states are constrained by other states (which are 'equally' sovereign), we cast doubt on the very idea of state sovereignty itself. If postmodernism involves a movement 'beyond' modernism (as its label suggests), then it must 'privilege' modernity (that is, acknowledge its centrality) in order to deconstruct the sovereign state.

Reworking liberalism – the relational argument

I mentioned earlier the bruising experience I had at an international conference in which a dismissive attitude to sovereignty was itself dismissed out of hand. But two points in particular stand out, and the reason why I remember them so vividly is that they offered a way forward – if only I had had the wit to take it!

The first was the observation that the sovereignty which I insisted on identifying with the state, had been conceived by John Stuart Mill as an attribute which individuals also enjoy. The second was a comment that I couched all my arguments in terms of the way everything is *related* to everything else. Hoffman's credo, one of the members of the group playfully remarked, is basically 'I relate, therefore I am'.

I can now see that the notion that sovereignty is an individual attribute provides the key to detaching sovereignty from the state. In Chapter 6 I note that some feminist scholars have spoken of a self-sovereignty which is clearly in tension with the sovereignty of the state. In Chapter 8 I argue that the notion of individual sovereignty arises from within the liberal tradition, and provides a crucial resource for developing a post-statist concept of sovereignty. The problem with individual sovereignty is that historically it has been conceived in a naturalist fashion, by which I mean that individuals are seen as having static natures which are not amenable to historical change. Hobbes, Locke and Rousseau, as classical liberals, all see individuals as private owners, both of themselves and of the property they acquire. Individuality is depicted in static and atomistic terms. This means that individuals inevitably come into collision with each other in ways which bring the force of the state into play. Individual sovereignty has to be complemented and underwritten by the sovereignty of the state.

It is true that later liberals abandon the concept of a state of nature and the idea of the state as a social contract. But in doing so, they simply move from a naturalistically conceived individual to a naturalistically conceived state. Any residual tension between the sovereignty of the individual and the sovereignty of the state disappears. At the same time, the acknowledgement that individuals have always lived in societies makes it possible to analyse the impact social life has upon individual sovereignty. Mill's argument in *On Liberty* is instructive in this regard.[7] For Mill not only explores the way in which social pressures influence the activity of individuals, but also challenges the idea that human nature is static and non-developmental. He raises the question whether individuals can have a sovereign right to end their sovereignty – a highly subversive point which implicitly challenges naturalistic conceptions of individual freedom.

Although liberalism accepts the need for the state, doctrines such as anarchism and Marxism do not. However, they argue for statelessness through naturalistic assumptions which make it inevitable that sovereign states continue to exist. Anarchists abstract the individual from society with notions of spontaneity and rebellion which identify government with the state, and force with coercion. Marxism, for its part, embraces notions of the proletariat, production and communism which have a naturalistic character, and therefore work against the emancipatory logic of a materialist method. Ironically, both anarchism and Marxism can only offer statist alternatives to the state, and hence the concept of sovereign individuality they adopt continues to have hierarchical and repressive overtones.

In Chapter 10 I seek to present a relational view of sovereignty which incorporates the insights of the arguments examined above but in a way which avoids their limitations. A relational view must in the first instance be realistic. It must relate to a real world in which sovereign states are prominent actors. The formal egalitarian norms upon which state sovereignty rests are central to the relational argument I adopt. If state sovereignty is a historical reality which affects all equally, then we cannot argue that some nations should settle for less than sovereign statehood, or that sovereign nations should be statist without at the same time having state sovereignty.

At the same time, we can only recognize state sovereignty as a reality if we begin to move beyond it. If sovereign states are to aspire to legitimacy, then they must identify sovereignty with the rights and capacities of individuals. But sovereign individuals can only be analysed in non-naturalist terms if we understand that identities are constructed through relationships. Relationships are historical, variable, contextual and multi-layered. Although modernists are right to present sovereignty as an absolute concept, an absolutist view of sovereignty can only be coherently sustained if it is not confined to particular periods, institutions or groupings. It is because relationships are multiple, dynamic and increasingly universal, that sovereignty is both absolute and relative in character.

In stretching itself vertically and horizontally, sovereignty also embraces human relationships with the wider world of nature. Human security is ecological security. Our relationships with ourselves and with others are only possible if we do not destroy the environment of which we are part. Humans can be sovereign on the condition that they respect all the elements of a universe affected by their relationships.

A relational view must avoid 'visions' of the world which are not rooted in realities. A 'utopian realism' needs to chart the way in which sovereign states themselves consolidate the common interests which make post-statist forms of conflict resolution effective. If sovereign statehood is to be 'realized', then it needs to address problems of violence, inequality and deprivation, and as it does so, sovereign statehood transforms itself into the governmental processes which allow individuals to exercise sovereignty. But the sovereign state can only be deconstructed, feminized and democratized, if we recognize it as an institution which has a central role to play in enabling sovereignty as self-government to become a reality.

Sticking with Sovereignty

The concept of sovereignty has entered the arena of public debate with a vengeance. It has become central to analysing global political developments in the world since the cold war, and in Britain the argument as to whether greater economic and political integration is desirable within the European Union (EU) pivots around the question of sovereignty. Will the adoption of a single currency involve the loss of British sovereignty? Or is a more integrated EU crucial to defending British interests and *therefore* (it is argued) British sovereignty?

Sovereignty is a highly contentious term. It is not only the politicians who argue about it. The concept provokes disagreement at an academic level as well.[1] But does that mean abandoning the term? I shall argue that we should stick with sovereignty: the fact that it is a contentious concept is not a reason for giving it up. The problem, I shall argue, arises with its linkage to the state. It is the state which generates a contention that is destructive and paralysing in character. To define sovereignty in a way in which contention serves as a stimulus to discussion rather than a source of paralysis, sovereignty needs to be separated from the state.

Introducing the abandonment thesis

The distinguished historian, E.H. Carr, writing before the Second World War, predicted that sovereignty would become increasingly blurred and indistinct as time went by. The problem, he argued, arose because the concept was forever being divided up, with distinctions made between political, legal, economic, external and internal sovereignty.[2] Jens Bartelson, who cites the words of Carr, also quotes Stanley Benn's protest, after the Second World War, that there were at least six different senses in which the term was being used. But despite these complaints, 'blurring' distinctions continue to proliferate. *National* sovereignty has been distinguished from *state* sovereignty, and in a recent text no less than *seven* distinct variants of the concept have been enumerated.[3]

The question then arises: if sovereignty has become increasingly ambiguous and nuanced, should we stop using the term? I shall call this argument the 'abandonment' thesis, and it is certainly Benn's view. Noting the discrepancies between the different uses that he painstakingly delineates, there is, he argues, a strong case 'for giving up so Protean a word'.[4] The ambiguity is such that the term would best be abandoned – precisely the conclusion reiterated by Raymond Aron some years later. Cynthia Weber also cites Ernst Haas to the same effect.[5] More recently, Michael Newman has concluded that sovereignty has become so distorted and ambiguous that the concept is 'now a barrier to analysis'.[6]

The bewildering ambiguity of sovereignty clearly signals the contestability of the concept. In W.B. Gallie's classic formulation, contestability arises when different meanings of the same term are expounded and evoked through conflicting sources of evidence, logic and rationality. But does it follow that because we can identify a concept as 'contested', we should therefore abandon it? Gallie identifies democracy as a contestable concept *par excellence*,[7] and the analogy with sovereignty is revealing. Both concepts embody a wide range of conflicting meanings, but is this a reason why we should stop using them?

The fact that sovereignty has become increasingly central to contemporary debate makes it all the more important that we seek to clarify it. While some may consider the whole notion anachronistic and irrelevant in the wake of developments within the EU such as the signing of the Maastricht Treaty in 1992,[8] others, quite rightly in my view, seek to retain the term. The analogy with democracy is a salient one. Like democracy, sovereignty is a concept which is positively evaluated from most (if not all) parts of the political spectrum. If this makes it ambiguous, it also makes it a conceptual challenge which we should not avoid.

It might be logically possible for the supporters, say, of a more integrated Europe to argue that because they favour a stronger EU, they oppose sovereignty. But this response is atypical. James had already noted in 1986 that support for the EU was normally pressed in terms of 'the greater sovereignty of a united Europe'. It has even been argued that increased involvement in, and sympathy for, the EU would increase British sovereignty, while Newman himself concedes that state sovereignty could actually be enhanced through Britain's integration with the EU.[9]

It is true that the acclaim that now generally surrounds sovereignty heightens the ambiguity of the term, and James has spoken rather dramatically of an 'intellectual quagmire' which threatens as contention over sovereignty intensifies.[10] But giving the term up simply because it is controversial means ignoring the preoccupations of political actors in the practical world. It also avoids tackling a question which is so often ignored: just why, and in what sense, is sovereignty a contentious political term?

The state and the abandonment thesis

I shall argue that the peculiarly contentious nature of sovereignty arises from its association with the state. F.H. Hinsley's classic analysis of sovereignty is premised on the assumption that the concept is 'closely linked with the nature, origin and history of the state'. In defining sovereignty as the idea that there is a 'final and absolute political authority in the community', he takes it for granted that this final and absolute community is a state. The state, he insists, is a necessary condition for the concept itself.[11]

Recent commentators agree. Bartelson argues that the discourse on sovereignty is so entangled with the question of the state, that it is impossible to define the state without embracing the question of sovereignty. Weber opens the first chapter of her book with the question: 'can one say anything about statehood without beginning by deciding what sovereignty means?' So closely linked are the two notions that she finds it legitimate to run them together as 'sovereign statehood' – the term which James also uses in his analysis of the concept.[12]

Sovereignty, I want to argue, is contentious because the state is contentious. David Easton explicitly links the elusive nature of the state with the elusive nature of sovereignty,[13] and after the Second World War Easton and his behaviouralist school of political theory abandoned the concept of the state and sovereignty. They were not

the only ones to do so. Linguistic analysts, in their quest for conceptual 'clarity', reached a similar conclusion. The state and sovereignty, they argued, were 'first order' problems which arose out of
political practice. They were not 'philosophically interesting' questions which required academic analysis. Some radical theorists supported the abandonment thesis for rather different reasons. The
concepts of state and sovereignty, they argued, had normative
implications which were too conservative in character!

All took the view that the concept of sovereignty should be abandoned because it is part and parcel of the elusiveness, partisanship
and abstractness of the state. Either state sovereignty conflicts with
the search for empirically testable and value-free hypotheses (the
behaviouralist position), or it gets in the way of conceptual purity
in our use of words (the contention of the linguistic analysts), or it
undermines the case for greater participation and control over our
lives (the argument of the radicals). Objections to the concept of
sovereignty might differ, but the conclusion was the same.[14]

Abandoning the abandonment thesis

Despite all these arguments, the case against the abandonment
thesis is a simple one. Sovereignty exists in the real world. To try
and ignore it is as futile as trying to ignore the existence of the state,
and when an argument developed in the 1980s for 'bringing the
state back in', this also ushered in a revival of interest in sovereignty. The point is that no protagonist of the abandonment thesis
has ever rejected the view that sovereignty and states exist. Elusive
and abstract they might be, but who can deny that sovereign states
still predominate in the world in which we live?

It is true that behaviouralists such as Easton sought in a relent-
lessly sustained way to expunge the notions of the state and sovereignty from political theory. But his own arguments demonstrate
graphically (if unwittingly) why state sovereignty, however vigor-
ously we push it out of the front door, inevitably slithers in through
the back. Instead of the state, Easton preferred to speak of the
political system which he defined as 'the authoritative allocation of
values for society as a whole'. But, as his critics pointed out, the idea
of authoritatively allocating values for society 'as a whole' only
makes sense if we assume that the political system is a sovereign
state.[15]

In his later work Easton defines the political system as an institution whose decisions are 'considered binding by most members
most of the time'.[16] But this still begs the question why decisions
which should be respected by everyone, are flouted by some.
Easton's problem is similar to that of his fellow behaviouralist,
Robert Dahl, who identifies an institution's exclusive right to use
force with 'the Government'.[17] For the point is that terminological
change does not do away with the institutional reality of the sovereign state. Indeed, Easton now concedes that the state was never
really left out of his analysis, and this point is echoed by behaviouralists and others elsewhere.[18] If institutions exist which claim
an exclusive and monopolistic right to regulate society's affairs
through force, then we are brought face to face with the reality of
sovereign states however we care to characterize them.

Some have argued that we should abandon the notion of sovereignty while still retaining the idea of the state. But a moment's
thought will reveal that this position is untenable. For while its protagonists contend that the state is too diverse, divided and erratic
to 'evoke as an entity', they do not deny that states exist.[19] If states
exist, then we may be sure that they will at least claim the right to
sovereignty. The failure to make a plausible case for abandoning
the state reinforces the need to persist with the problem of sovereignty, however contentious, ambiguous and elusive the term might
be. Trying to avoid speaking of sovereignty while states still exist
simply lets the concept in, as Bartelson has noted, by default.[20]

Introducing the indefinability thesis

Some theorists are willing to stick with sovereignty, but they argue
that while the term should not be abandoned, it is impossible to
define. I call this the 'indefinability thesis', and it is advanced in particular by those who can be described as postmodernists or post-
structuralists.

The kind of postmodernists I have in mind accept the contestable
nature of sovereignty,[21] and they see the link with the state as the
source of the contention and ambiguity that have made sovereignty
such a problematic concept. Bartelson, for example, argues that
whether we look at realist and neo-realist international theory,
macrosociology with its emphasis upon state formation, or the position of those (such as Anthony Giddens) who seek to synthesize

structure and agency in their social analysis, all are mesmerized
(and here Bartelson quotes Martin Wight) by the 'intellectual
prejudice of the sovereign state'.[22]

But if postmodernists are correct to link the contentious character of sovereignty with the state, why do some insist that the concept
is indefinable? Weber takes the view that, rather than ask what sovereignty means in itself, we should examine the way in which theorists and diplomats 'stabilize' this meaning when states intervene in
the affairs of others. When we speak of sovereignty, all we can point
to are the particular definitions which states use to constitute themselves as sovereign entities. There is no 'real' or 'true' meaning of
sovereignty as such.[23] Bartelson concurs. The concept of sovereignty is tied to the idea of knowledge, and what we mean by knowledge depends upon what we understand by existence. Sovereignty
decides. To be sovereign is to determine what is knowable, what is
true and what exists. Since sovereignty is the *precondition* for our
knowing things, it cannot, Bartelson argues, be part of knowledge
itself. As 'a question tacitly implied in the very practice of questioning', it is a concept which is impossible to define.[24]

Bartelson likens sovereignty to Kant's notion of the parergon in
aesthetic discourse as the frame which does the framing. Since sovereignty constitutes the basis of knowledge and truth, it cannot be
part of that which it establishes. It is the precondition of all
'essences', and therefore has no essence itself. Instead of trying to
say what sovereignty *is*, we should examine what happens when
others try to answer this question.[25]

Sovereignty and meaning

The problems which Weber and Bartelson raise in defence of their
indefinability thesis are illuminating because they are problems
which confront us when we link sovereignty to the state. Weber
graphically demonstrates just what an extraordinary institution the
state is.

If we define sovereignty in terms of the state, she argues, then we
necessarily refer to 'the absolute authority a state holds over a territory and people'. The state 'represents' the people over which it has
authority, and these people constitute a territorial community
which is identified in terms of its boundaries. But the authority of
the state is continuously challenged as people break laws, and the

territorial boundaries identifying the community are ceaselessly transgressed as illegal migrants (for example) enter societies in which they are not supposed to dwell.[26] In other words, defining sovereignty as a clearly bounded and law-abiding community represented by a state is highly problematic, and Weber seeks to 'undefine' sovereignty (as she puts it) by providing a critique of the whole idea of representation. The state functionaries who claim to represent the popular community, she argues, construct the very community which they purport to represent. A 'self-referential' absurdity is involved. This is not simply the absurdity of a concept. It is the absurdity of the sovereign practice of states. But if, as Weber argues, the state is absurd (and I believe that it is), why should we not incorporate this absurdity into the way in which we *define* sovereignty itself?

Weber and Bartelson are opposed to definitions – to all definitions – because definitions, they argue, imply a 'representational' relationship between language and existence. The very practice of defining a term, Bartelson says, assumes that language is a transparent medium which can represent that which takes place in the world outside the knowing subject. Whether sovereignty represents a reality 'out there' or is simply a set of juridical rules for identifying independent states, it embraces institutions which are fluid and ambiguous. This fluidity and ambiguity makes sovereignty contentious. As a source of theoretical confusion and a site of political struggle, it is impossible to define.[27]

But while Bartelson and Weber are certainly right to argue that we should not abandon contentious issues, how can we tackle these issues unless we seek to define them? This dilemma is present in Gallie's original formulation of the 'contestability' problem, for Gallie himself argues that we have no way of evaluating the competing merits of contestable concepts. As John Gray has noted, 'there seems to be a radical fault in the very notion of a contest which cannot by its nature be won or lost'.[28] Gallie's argument is curiously defeatist and relativistic. The indefinability thesis may seem at variance with the 'value-freedom' and conceptual purism of behavioural and linguistic positions, but in practice it embraces a similar kind of positivism. If, as Bartelson and Weber argue, we can never do more than analyse the definitions of others, then this means that we are powerless to make substantial judgements for ourselves.

Once again . . . the problem of the state

Postmodernists such as Bartelson and Weber find themselves
trapped within the numbing confines of the indefinability thesis
because they see no way of separating sovereignty from the state. It
is true that Weber (co-editing a volume with Thomas Biersteker)
has referred recently to the need to separate state and sovereignty,
but this is precisely what she fails to do. The relationship between
the state and sovereignty is described as 'mutually constitutive' and
when the two are 'provisionally defined', they appear to presuppose
each other.[29]

It is not enough to note that the state is a contentious concept
which lies at the source of sovereignty's conceptual problems. We
have to define both the state and sovereignty in a way which makes
it possible to separate them. While the proponents of the indefinability thesis correctly observe that the contentiousness of the state
paralyses our conceptualization of sovereignty, they assume at the
same time that sovereignty cannot exist outside the state. The state
is taken as given. This has two consequences. It means that the only
form of sovereignty conceivable is *state* sovereignty, and that when
sovereignty is linked to knowledge and meaning, this linkage is presented in (what I want to call) a statist way.

By this I mean that those who support the indefinability thesis
adopt a top-down view of the material world. They see this world
as an anarchic, shapeless mass which requires concepts to order it.
If institutions are fluid and ambiguous, then, so the argument runs,
they cannot be defined. This defeatist conclusion flows from the
assumption that ideas act in state-like fashion in creating order and
existence: the real world is but the servant and slave of our 'defining' concepts. The notion of sovereignty as a parergon (revealingly
borrowed from Kant) presents the state as a mystical creator which
is the condition for all that is created. It is the *source* of meaning
and therefore not part of this meaning itself.

But why should we assume that the real world depends for its
existence upon ideas in this top-down fashion? If, as Bartelson comments, debates about sovereignty have been bedevilled by the intellectual prejudice of the sovereign state, then surely this is the
prejudice we must tackle if the contention surrounding sovereignty
is to be resolved. Only if we can conceptualize sovereignty in a way

which looks beyond the state, will the question of contention itself cease to be a barrier to definition.

Here it is helpful to note that 'contention' can be used in two quite different senses. On the one hand, contention can be seen as a stimulus to theory when it encourages us to resolve problems. On the other hand, it becomes a source of paralysis when it leads to the despairing conclusion that concepts are indefinable. In the first sense sovereignty remains contentious since political theory is ultimately linked to political practice, and people will naturally take differing views as to how they should govern their lives. Whatever definition of sovereignty we adopt will arouse controversy. Political concepts are contentious simply because all theoretical vocabularies have a practical bite which affects people's interests.

Why, then, is contention seen as a reason for declaring concepts to be indefinable? It is here that contention in the second sense – contention as a negative and destructive force – comes into play. The state, in my view, is the source of the problem. As long as we assume that sovereignty can only take a statist form, contention will paralyse rather than act as a stimulus. Hence, this book seeks to detach sovereignty from the state. I will argue that the state is a contradictory institution which uses force to secure community so that it ultimately works to prevent rather than facilitate debate. Its absurdity is encapsulated in the fact that it asserts a monopoly of legitimate force which it does not (and cannot) possess.[30]

It follows that the state can and must be defined. Of course, defining the state involves a certain irony since when we define the state, we necessarily highlight its problematic character as an institution whose contentious character paralyses rather than stimulates controversy. The contentiousness of the state is therefore different in kind from the contentiousness which facilitates debate. The one is positive, the other negative. We can only move beyond the paralysing contentiousness of the state as a concept if we move beyond the state as a troubled institutional reality.

The same is not true of sovereignty. What makes sovereignty an impossibly problematic concept is the fact that it is linked to the state. Contentiousness paralyses the concept of sovereignty as long as we take the state for granted, unthinkingly importing its absolutist and top-down perspectives into our analysis of concepts. Once we detach sovereignty from the state, we can then define it as a concept which denotes empowerment and development – a concept which embraces democracy, autonomy and self-government. When sovereignty is separated from the state, contention remains, but it is no longer conceptually paralysing.

3
Realism and the State

We have assumed thus far that sovereignty is a contentious concept. Although this assumption is supported by those who would either abandon the term or refuse to define it, it is denied by a third position that also deserves our attention. This position can be identified with the realist school in international relations (IR). It accepts the argument that contentious concepts should be abandoned but it seeks to define sovereignty precisely because it believes that it is possible to rescue the concept from contention.

Realism still represents the prevailing orthodoxy in the discipline of IR.[1] It is important, partly because it is still so influential, but also because its attempt to free sovereignty from contention spectacularly fails. This failure, as we will see from a detailed assessment of Alan James's argument, is most instructive. Realists place the state at the heart of their analysis. In this way they unwittingly reveal why the concept of sovereignty has been seen as impossibly contentious and paralysingly problematic. Implicitly at least, they reinforce the point which lies at the heart of this book. If sovereignty is to be explored as a coherent and meaningful concept, it has to be detached from the state.

Introducing the separatist thesis

Realists embrace what I wish to call a 'separatist' thesis since they argue that sovereignty can be 'separated' from the contention which would otherwise make the term impossible to define. They take the view, however, that a non-contentious view of sovereignty is only possible if we rigorously restrict our attention to the activity of states as external or international actors.

To understand the realist position, we need to make sense of a curious proposition which has been advanced by some post-modernist writers on sovereignty. R.J.B. Walker argues that sovereignty is an essentially *un*contested concept whose meaning is only 'marginally contestable by constitutional lawyers and other connoisseurs of fine lines'. These sentiments are not only endorsed by Weber, but also echoed in Bartelson's comment that sovereignty is 'essentially uncontested as the foundation of modern political discourse'. What is contested, he argues, is the meaning of sovereignty within the same discourse.[2]

The argument sounds bizarre. How can sovereignty be both contested and uncontested at the same time? Realists accept that sovereignty is contestable for those who find the concept either empirically untestable, philosophically uninteresting, or normatively unacceptable. The point is that these thinkers all tackle the concept within the confines of political theory, and therein lies the rub. To realists, as I have identified them, IR is a discipline which stands outside political theory. Hence, while they sympathize with those who would abandon the concepts of the state and sovereignty within domestic political theory, they contend that this stance does not affect students of IR in the same way. The distinction between IR on the one hand and political theory on the other arises out of a distinction between what is domestic and what is international. The contention which blights the former need not paralyse the latter. Sovereignty might be contentious in political theory, but it can be rescued from this contention within IR.

Behaviouralism and the two faces of the state

The behaviouralist position is particularly illuminating in this regard. On the one hand (as I have argued in Chapter 2), behaviouralists press for a particularly vigorous version of the abandonment thesis by presenting the political system as a conceptual substitute for the state. On the other hand, they accept a statist focus for IR.

Easton graphically exemplifies this equivocation when he comments that the state has led a double life. While its usage within internal politics ought to be abandoned, the term has never disappeared as a concept for identifying the 'unified actors in the international arena'. Here all continue to recognize the concept as a legitimate abbreviation for the nation state.[3] This suggests that if the sovereign state has become intensely problematic in internal or domestic politics, it has remained uncontestable within IR.

The behaviouralists, in other words, have a contradictory view of the state. The state is seen as ideological, ambiguous, elusive and incoherent. Yet they also accept that states are key actors on the international scene. Thus Kaplan, as the major architect of behaviouralism in IR, identifies his key variables in terms of *states*. Although he and Bull fiercely debated the respective merits of behaviouralism and classical IR theory, both assumed that states are the most important actors within IR.[4]

The contradictory attitude of the behavouralists is borne out in J.P. Nettl's oft-cited argument for the state 'as a conceptual variable'. Writing in 1967, Nettl links the state with sovereignty as concepts which have both fallen out of favour. Yet Nettl also argues that whatever the state may or may not be internally, 'there have been few challenges to both its sovereignty *and* its autonomy in "foreign affairs" '. A concept which is highly contestable within societies seems perfectly straightforward when sandwiched between them. The United Kingdom and the United States may be stateless domestically, but they are uncontestably statist and sovereign in their international relations.[5]

The arguments of Easton and Nettl are echoed by James when he contends that what has plunged the concept of sovereignty into an intellectual quagmire is a focus on the internal nature of the state. Political thinkers, he comments, have failed to provide a lucid, no-nonsense definition of sovereignty because they have 'almost always been directing themselves to the domestic political scene'. Hence James comments – rather remarkably! – that in analysing sovereignty, 'the work of the political theorists will find no place' in his work.[6] A neat, crisp and above all uncontentious solution to the problem requires that we focus exclusively on the external dimensions of the state.

The state-centric view of politics

But why, it may be asked, is the analysis of sovereignty and the state within the international realm not itself a task for political theory?

The realist argument is rooted in a state-centric view of politics. If we accept the assumption that the sovereign state captures the essence of the political process then, strictly speaking, there can be no politics outside the state. A theory of politics is, and can only be, a theory of the state.

When Wight famously raised the question why there is no international theory, his answer was basically that political theory is 'the tradition of speculation about the state'. A *theory* of inter-state relations is not really possible unless we assume that a world state can be forged in which the sovereignty of the national state is reproduced at the international level. Since realists take the view (and on this it is difficult to disagree with them) that such a development is neither possible nor desirable, we necessarily return to Wight's somewhat provocative point that a *theory* of relationships between states is impossible, since the state itself stands at the heart of political theory.[7]

A state-centric view of sovereignty is necessarily linked to the conceptualization of the international order as *anarchy*. Anarchy arises because, in Wight's oft-cited formulation, there is a 'multiplicity of independent sovereign states acknowledging no political superior'. Anarchy here has a 'theoretical' as well as a practical meaning. The international realm is also anarchic because it is not possible, realists argue, to theorize about that which lies beyond the state. Community, as Walker puts it, is seen to lie only within the state as the limit of our political imagination. It is 'eternally absent' between states.[8] An analysis of inter-state relations can and should dispense with political theory as such.

It might be argued that this is an impossible position to sustain. If it were literally true that the international system cannot be theorized, then nothing could be said about it even as a system of 'anarchy'. But realism, it is worth noting, manifests a curious kind of consistency here even if, as we shall argue, its search for an uncontentious view of sovereignty ultimately fails. For *if* we assume that political theory is about the state as a domestic actor, then it follows that the study of IR is not itself theoretical in character.

The point is that, as far as realists are concerned, the sovereign state is here to stay. In James's view, the debate over the EU does not in itself raise the question of sovereign statehood. Even if the identity of each member state were to be submerged within a new union, he argues, that would simply mean that where there had been many sovereign states before, now there would only be one. What is developing in Europe, he comments (in a work edited with Robert Jackson), is no more than the embryo of a European state which (at best) would mean 'a realignment and an endorsement and not a superannuation of sovereign statehood'. Plus ça change, plus c'est la même chose.[9]

The state as an abstraction

Despite his attempt to keep political theory at bay, James appears to concede the theoretical nature of his own analysis. He comments that the object to which the word 'sovereignty' refers is 'notional in character'. No one has ever seen a sovereign state 'except in the eye of the mind'. Academics, James says, have the task of 'teasing out plausible generalities about the nature of life at the international level'.[10] But this is precisely the problem. For these 'generalities' merely refer to multiple replicas of the same unit – the sovereign state – so that, conceptually speaking, sovereign states are all identical in character.

Realists depict the international realm as a world in which *the* state is replicated in plural form. Yet states clearly differ in the particular way they relate to their own past, to their domestic societies, to other states and to international actors of a non-statist kind. Realists strip away all these differentiating features, leaving us with sovereign states which are identical with one another. They emphasize only the 'sameness' of states, and it is this level of abstraction which makes a political theory of inter-state relations appear problematic.

It is true that Wight seems to retreat from the assertion that there is no international theory when he allows for an IR 'theory' of the balance of power. 'Realistically' conceived, however, the concept of the balance of power encapsulates a world in which sovereign states are all identical. In Hans Morgenthau's realist account of IR, the behaviour of states is linked to a concept of human nature which expresses itself in terms of 'elemental bio-psychological' drives to live, propagate and dominate. The point is that these drives are common 'to all men' – human nature is the same everywhere and at all times – and therefore we encounter in individual form the same statist behaviour noted at the international level.

Morgenthau himself makes this linkage clear when he asserts that states exercise their sovereignty according to 'a general social principle to which all societies composed of a number of autonomous units owe the autonomy of their component parts'.[11]

Autonomy here denotes 'sameness', so that if by theory we mean a capacity to understand something in a *specific* relationship to something else, realists have a point when they deny the theoretical character of their own arguments. They are not, after all, concerned with the way in which the particular identity of the sovereign state is moulded by its relationships with 'others' – the citizens subject to the force of domestic law; the weaker states bullied and cajoled in the international arena; the transnational organizations which impinge upon states with their economic and moral concerns. In so far as realists consider other factors in their analysis of the sovereign state – power, human nature, interests, force, and so on – these factors serve not to differentiate but merely to reinforce the 'sameness' of states.

But don't some realists make judgements which involve differentiating states from one another? Morgenthau was to argue that the USA's policy on Vietnam was not in either country's 'national interest', while Waltz, a major figure in the realist canon, makes it clear that we should not assume that states necessarily succeed in perpetuating their own security. In applying their general ideas to specific events, as Smith points out, realists often employ conceptions of power which are far more nuanced than their position would seem to allow.[12] But the logic of realism is clear nevertheless – it is unambiguously statist and militantly abstract in character.

It is therefore difficult to disagree with Rosenberg when he complains that realists define the state as 'ontologically anterior to the international system'. The sovereign state is simply there, and because differences within states, between states and with non-state actors, are conceptually excluded, a critical theory of state sovereignty is not possible. Realism, Rosenberg comments, 'mimics the vocabulary of the state's rationalization of its own behaviour'.[13] Its uncritical and abstract view of the state makes realism a kind of theory of non-theory. It embraces a positivist conception of the world in which state sovereignty is merely noted, but never subject to critique. It is a theoretical position which, as we shall see, is impossible to sustain.

James's no-nonsense definition: form without content?

James, it has been said, expounds the realist approach in IR with 'admirable consistency'.[14] The clarity and sharpness of his argument make it a compelling example of what a state-centric view of sovereignty looks like in the realist tradition.

When we focus on 'the practice of states' as external actors, James argues, contention disappears. The actions of states make the meaning of sovereignty 'plain'. Sovereignty is that which allows a state to be eligible for admission to international society. While entities called 'states' may exist as non-sovereign bodies within federal institutions such as the USA, only states with sovereign attributes qualify for what James calls 'international actorhood'.[15] Sovereignty involves constitutional independence or separateness. While international law may give rise to sovereign rights, these are only rights given to states which are *already* sovereign. The point is that sovereignty is an aspect of a state's nature 'which is quite independent of its relations with others'.

James argues that constitutional independence involves neither parity of economic or military power, nor indeed political independence if by this is meant a capacity to ignore external constraint. All that is implied is that, in terms of constitutional law, the sovereign state is 'in control of its own destiny' – 'a clear and straightforward reflection of the fact that it is constitutionally independent'.[16] If, in James's view, we were to identify sovereignty with 'substantive' factors such as loyalty, legitimacy, democratic institutions, military prowess, or the rule of law, then the kind of contention and ambiguity which has bedevilled discussions of sovereignty within a domestic context, would necessarily return.

Hence the argument for sovereignty has to be explicitly formalist in character. Membership of the UN may be a consequence of sovereignty, but it is not a criterion for it. States are still sovereign even when they are subject to the legal constraints imposed by regional and international bodies to which they belong. Indeed, even puppet states can be 'sovereign' since in formal terms they are constitutionally independent. The point is that 'sovereignty, while it does not usually end in formalities, always starts there'.[17]

The problem, however, is this. In a world in which sovereign states come and go, do we not have to say something about how states acquire sovereignty in the first place? James finds it tempting to avoid this question. He argues that 'in most circumstances' the question of identifying sovereignty is a straightforward matter of 'factually' pointing to those states which are constitutionally independent.[18] However, as we shall now see, in situations when sovereignty is *explicitly* contested, the need to move beyond 'form' becomes irresistible.

Sovereignty as a physical reality

To his credit, James does tackle cases where doubt about sovereignty has arisen. States exist which are subject to what James calls international 'aversion', and this aversion is evident in relation to divided states such as the two Germanies during the cold war; pariah states such as South Africa and its 'independent' homelands in the years of apartheid; or illegal states such as Ian Smith's Rhodesia (which only lasted from 1965 to 1979). In James's view, states such as these can still be said to be sovereign since, 'factually speaking', they enjoyed constitutional independence. Sovereignty 'expresses a legal and not a physical reality'.[19]

But what happens in situations where legal realities are themselves disputed? Take the case of Smith's Rhodesia. This is a state which was not recognized by any other in the 14 years of its existence, and James concedes that the Smith regime came into existence in an unlawful manner. The Rhodesian case is important for it compels James to shift his conceptual ground. While he rejects the view that sovereignty depends upon international recognition, he argues that a sovereign state's continued existence will ultimately depend upon its ability to keep its enemies at bay. 'The ultimate point is rarely reached but, if it is, the legal claim to sovereignty will be as nothing in the absence of an ability to defend it by force of arms.' Sovereignty, in other words, is rooted in a kind of statist effectiveness which rests upon 'a significant congruence between the decisions of those who purport to rule and the actual behaviour of their alleged subjects'.[20]

Viewed in this light, James argues, there can be 'little doubt that a new sovereign state had emerged bearing the name of Rhodesia'. The Smith regime may not have been legal but it was effective. On the one hand, James speaks of the state as 'a legal expression of a physical reality'. On the other hand, it appears that should a collision between the two occur, it is ultimately the physical reality – the capacity to exercise force – which matters.[21] This point is crucial to understanding how states both acquire and lose sovereignty.

Why was it possible for Bangladesh to emerge as a new sovereign state in 1971? The failure of the Pakistani forces in the East to exercise effective power was decisive. Why didn't Biafra – to take another of James's examples – become a sovereign state? Again his point is a 'substantive' one. Ultimately, the federal government in Nigeria had 'superior strength' over the Biafran rebels.[22] James's own argument demonstrates that it is impossible to sustain a purely formal-legal (that is, an apparently non-contentious) view of sovereignty. For if form depends upon substance and substance turns fundamentally upon the capacity of the state to impose rule (by force of arms if need be), then all those factors which relate to this 'physical reality' are crucial in accounting for the presence of sovereignty.

James is vulnerable to the accusation that his position tends to degenerate into mere apologia. To suggest that the Smith regime in Rhodesia was sovereign because of the 'significant congruence' it secured between rulers and ruled, rather downplays the use of terror, emergency laws and the explicit absence of democratic institutions involved in attaining this 'congruence'. In trying to abstract form from content, James cannot avoid exaggerating the stability and permanence of illegitimate and undemocratic regimes. Thus (writing in the mid-1980s) he finds it is hard to see the homelands policy being abandoned in South Africa, although he does concede (rather cautiously) that apartheid 'may be less emphasised in the future'.[23] But there is no hint here that, just four years after his book was published, Mandela would be released and the African National Congress involved in negotiations for a democratic South Africa!

To say, in similar vein, that 'as of early 1985, sovereignty for the Eritreans looks as far away as ever, as it does for the Kurds, the Basques and many other such groups'[24] again demonstrates the limitations of an argument which in the name of realism, simply projects the existing *status quo* as a permanent political landscape.

The state and contention

James's analysis is important because it demonstrates how the problematic character of sovereignty is tied to the problematic character of the state. He concedes that sovereignty as formal constitutional independence, has to be underpinned by a 'physical reality' which allows the state a greater capacity to enforce a greater 'congruence' between ruler and ruled than any acknowledged rival.

Smith has argued that Max Weber's view of politics, the state and international relations established the discourse of the realist approach.[25] The problems which arise from Weber's definition of the state are precisely those which also affect James's realist analysis of sovereignty. Even a state whose institutions have 'collapsed' (as in the case of the Congo in the 1960s or Lebanon in the 1980s) is still sovereign, in James's view, as long it is not formally subject to another's constitutional embrace.[26] James's definition of sovereignty is premised on the assumption that the state's claim to exercise a monopoly of legitimate force may be highly imperfect and partial.

The point can be expressed a little more sharply. States, as I have commented earlier, assert a monopoly of legitimate force which they do not and cannot possess. The very claim to possess a monopoly of legitimate force presupposes the existence of rival claims by 'competitors' of an international as well as a domestic kind. No matter! All that is required for sovereignty in James's definition is that there is some kind of functioning state, however divided its people and partial its order. Yet it is not difficult to see that every state suffers from a contradictory identity, and this problematic identity cannot be excluded through the kind of formalism which James tries to sustain in his definition of sovereignty. When deconstructed, his own argument reveals that without a certain physical reality – a capacity to impose order by force – state sovereignty loses even its formal status as a constitutionally independent entity. States attempt to impose order through force. In so doing, they demonstrate their contradictory character as institutions seeking a monopoly they can never attain. The activity of states themselves indicates why it is impossible to insulate the discussion of sovereignty from the ambiguities and uncertainties of political theory.

In defending his formal definition, James argues that the sovereignty of the state has nothing to do with political independence, autonomy, impermeability, or lack of external constraint. Sovereignty implies neither legitimacy nor human rights. The sovereign state has no necessary link with morality, democracy, civil or political rights. Indeed, sovereignty is not even tied to order and security since the term, as he defines it, 'is by no means the recipe for a safe and prosperous life, nor for internal stability'.[27]

This argument, however, does not make his realist view of sovereignty less contentious. It merely shows just how contradictory the state really is. It is an institution whose unifying theory presupposes a divisive practice. If we *do* want order, justice, rights, democracy and legitimacy then, as James makes clear, we cannot look to state sovereignty to provide them. For sovereignty, as the legal expression of a physical reality, is tied to the problematic character of the state. It is the state that lies at the root of sovereignty's numbing ambiguity and elusiveness.

The realist argument within IR eloquently if unwittingly testifies, therefore, to the need to detach sovereignty from the state. This is the only way to secure a definition of sovereignty which is coherent and consistent.

The Problem of Modernity

I have argued thus far that sovereignty can only be coherently defined if it is detached from the state. But it might be objected that it is unnecessary to detach sovereignty from the state as such, since sovereignty is the product of the modern state alone.

I call this the 'modernist' thesis, and I shall look in particular at Rosenberg's Marxian variant of this argument and Hinsley's classic case for sovereignty as a feature of the modern state. I will argue that the modernist notion of sovereignty, as a unitary, indivisible and absolute power concentrated in the state, represents a significant historical advance over earlier and more 'pluralistic' notions. At the same time, the modernist view of sovereignty brings to a head the impossibly contentious nature of this 'bothersome' concept, and therefore ironically modernity lays the basis for the post-statist concept of sovereignty which I am concerned to develop.

Rosenberg's historical critique and the problem of difference

Rosenberg argues that realism fails to sustain a historically sensitive view of the state, and that, as a consequence, it is unable to identify sovereignty as a specifically modern phenomenon. The first proposition is valid but, it seems to me, the second is vulnerable and one-sided.

Rosenberg contends that realists view states (along with markets and individuals) as 'natural starting points'. If we are to *de*naturalize entities, we need to see them in a process of change, and, to do this, an explicit recognition of their historical distinctiveness is crucial.[1] In challenging the realists' lack of historicity, Rosenberg is right to stress just how different states are – how different, for example, the medieval and ancient worlds are to the modern world of mercantile and industrial capitalism. If we compare the funeral oration of Pericles, so often cited by realists as a timeless exposition of power, with the speech of the Venetian doge on the resources of his city in 1421, we encounter radical discontinuities between ancient Greek and medieval Italian cities. The Greek *polis* knew nothing of the structural antagonism of town and country, and pursued a militarist logic of accumulation alien to the commercially-minded Italians.[2]

Rosenberg is surely correct to emphasize that an analysis of the state and sovereignty must focus on the centrality of change. But to do this, we require a view of history which embraces both similarity and difference. In order to see the way in which sovereignty arises, it is important to understand how the 'same' entity expresses itself differently in different historical periods. Rosenberg's problem is that in opposition to the abstract continuity adopted by the realists, he stresses an equally abstract discontinuity. He argues that in ancient Greece there was no state, and that while medieval polities were *states*, these states were not sovereign because monarchs had to share jurisdiction with the church and nobility. Sovereignty, in his view, only comes about when the rise of a capitalist division of labour makes it possible for the state to be 'abstracted' as a 'purely political' public institution.[3]

Accepting an illusion

There is no doubt that under capitalism, the extraction of a surplus appears to be the private activity of individuals rather than the public activity of the state. Rosenberg draws upon Marx to good effect to argue that the individual egalitarianism within a capitalist society is a modern phenomenon which masks the domination of property. This, as Rosenberg points out, is not merely a domestic question: the internal 'invisible hand' of the 'domestic' market expresses itself internationally as a balance of power between seemingly impersonal, anonymous and abstractly equal states.[4]

But it does not follow that because the capitalist state is different from its predecessors, it alone can be said to have sovereignty.

While it is true that under capitalism the state appears to stand outside of society, this – as Rosenberg himself acknowledges – is an *illusion*. States, despite their 'purely political' status, continue to regulate society, police contracts, raise taxes and mould the processes of production. They are also increasingly porous and interdependent within a global context.[5] Under liberal capitalism, sovereignty becomes unprecedentedly paradoxical. But the critical force of Rosenberg's argument is lost if we insist that sovereignty is a purely 'political' phenomenon confined to a capitalist system. For once sovereignty is defined in this way, deceptive and illusory appearances are taken at face value. The whole point about Marx's analysis is that sovereignty is not a purely political phenomenon, since abstract appearances and institutional separations conceal the concrete involvement of the sovereign state with the economy and society.

Moreover Marx assumes, as Rosenberg's own quotations make clear, that sovereignty is capable of taking different historical forms, and that under capitalism, sovereignty is characterized by the abstract egalitarianism of market relationships. If, however, the purely political character of the liberal state is illusory and misleading, how then can these deceptive appearances form the basis for a definition of sovereignty?[6]

Differentiating state sovereignty: antiquity and feudalism

At this point it is useful to examine the arguments of Hinsley for, like Rosenberg, he tries to define sovereignty simply in terms of the modern state. Hinsley takes the view that although the state is necessary for sovereignty, it is not sufficient.

Sovereignty, he argues, requires the state to be accepted by its subjects. This implies that subject and state are distinct. At the same time, if sovereign power is to reside in the political community, this power must be absolute and illimitable. The 'body politic' (that is, the state and society) constitutes 'a single personality' composed of rulers and ruled alike.[7] Hinsley accepts that in ancient Greek thought, the state is conceived as having supreme power. But this supremacy does not equate with sovereignty since the citizen is not seen as distinct from, and therefore having the capacity to agree to, the state.[8]

But why should we assume that sovereignty can only exist in a modern form? It is true that sovereignty is *explicitly* formulated in the modern period, and Andrew Vincent is right to argue that the concept was not known 'in all its fullness' before the fifteenth and sixteenth centuries.[9] But it does not follow that the reality of state sovereignty did not exist in earlier periods, even though the concept itself had yet to be formulated. The point – as we have already noted in our critique of Rosenberg – is that we need to stress both continuity and discontinuity in the development of state sovereignty. Many of the attributes within Greek, Roman or medieval thought were subsequently integrated into the modernist conception of sovereignty. Indeed, as Charles Merriam has pointed out, Aristotle's argument that there must be supreme power in the state is enough to establish the idea of sovereignty in his theory.[10] Once we identify the existence of a supreme power – the power of life and death – in rulers, then not only can we point to the presence not only of the state in pre-modern societies (as Hinsley acknowledges), but also of *sovereignty*.

Hinsley's contention, however, is that kingdoms and empires (while undeniably statist in character) cannot be seen as sovereign since in pre-modern polities the ruler is not linked to a particular society. As a personal and theocratic figure, he (and it is invariably a 'he') holds sway over numerous communities and varied peoples. While the Roman Empire does see the emergence of a single central authority above the law, even here, Hinsley argues, absolute and final authority is still limited. The celebrated formulation – 'whatever pleases the prince has the force of law' – is qualified by the fact that the power to declare the existence of law is transferred to the prince by the people.[11]

Yet, as far as Merriam is concerned, this dictum that the ruler is the source of law – the *legibus solutus* doctrine – contains the idea of sovereignty in 'its clearest expression', while Vincent sees it as a formulation of public power 'later to be linked to sovereignty'.[12] For Hinsley and the protagonists of the modernity thesis, however, supremacy is not enough. Theocracy in Islam, Hinsley argues, cannot be said to embody sovereignty since it is God rather than the earthly ruler who is all-powerful. For the same reason the Pope in Christian Europe was not sovereign, because the canon law by which he ruled was simply a morality which recognized no distinction between religious, political and social fields.[13]

There is no doubt that feudalism lacked a conception of a unified and all-embracing sovereignty vested exclusively in a state ruler. But the point is that state sovereignty can exist even though a *conception* of absolute and illimitable state power has yet to develop. Thus Perry Anderson can refer to 'the pyramidal, parcellized *sovereignty* of medieval social formations with their estates and liege systems'. Moreover, he makes the crucial point that the Pope's assertion of supreme power within the church set the precedent for the later pretensions of secular princes.[14] This is why it is appropriate, in my view, to employ not only a broad notion of the state (as Hinsley does) but also a broad notion of sovereignty.

Vincent speaks of a popular and group sovereignty nourished by the communal life of towns and guilds from the thirteenth century 'although the proponents would not have used the appellation "sovereignty"'. Hinsley himself concedes that we could use modern terminology to say that God and the law were sovereign in the medieval community. However, 'such terminology is wholly inappropriate to the political character of the communities and to the medieval idea of law'.[15] But why? If law and indeed statehood can take traditional and archaic forms, why can't sovereignty as well?

The centralization of power which undoubtedly occurs as we move towards the modern state, builds upon earlier notions of sovereignty. Anderson comments that the revival of interest in Roman law, with its conception of unconditional private property and imperial sovereignty, allowed late feudal rulers to work towards greater territorial integration and administrative and legal centralization.[16] The concept of sovereignty in ancient and medieval states may have been inchoate, embryonic and undeveloped, but it does not follow that sovereignty *as a political reality* was not involved in the power struggles of the medieval period.

Merriam's comment on St Thomas Aquinas's political thought is revealing in this regard. In Aquinas, Merriam argues, 'a strong doctrine on the nature of sovereignty' was hindered by the idea that divine and natural law prevailed over positive law. But the point is that a 'weak' doctrine of sovereignty still hinges on notions of supremacy and the absolute power of the state. Hinsley says of the Thomists (followers of Aquinas) that 'if any authority was sovereign in their scheme, it was God alone'. We are not denying that the modern view of sovereignty, like the modern state, offers a secular rather than a religious basis for authority. We are merely arguing, as Kathleen Jones does, that we can speak of a medieval view of sovereignty. How else are we to characterize a power which connected 'different stations of the social order in an organic web of hierarchically defined patterns of superordination and subordination', and which depended upon 'appeals to a concept of authority as the ultimate source of legitimate rule'?[17]

Hinsley (like Rosenberg) is correct to stress the distinctive character of modern sovereignty. In its modernist conception, sovereignty explicitly celebrates the concentration of power within a particular state. But this important historical insight is mystified if we insist that this particular form is identical to sovereignty as such. Since earlier conceptions of political power were also statist and supremacist, we are entitled to speak of them as embodying sovereignty as well.[18]

Bodin and the modernist conception of sovereignty

Commentators generally agree that the sixteenth-century French thinker, Jean Bodin, was the first to conceptualize sovereignty in a systematic manner. What is significant about Bodin's position is the fact, in Hinsley's view, that he integrated both ruler and ruled in a way in which they had not been integrated before.[19]

This point helps us to understand why the modernist conception of sovereignty is so profoundly problematic in character. Bodin identifies sovereignty as the power of a ruler to impose laws on subjects regardless of their consent. However, he also argues that sovereign kings were subject to divine and natural law, and were to respect the rights and liberties of free subjects. He even took the view that in France except in emergencies, new taxation required the consent of the Estates – otherwise property rights would be violated.[20]

This raises the celebrated problem of consistency. Was it illogical for Bodin to argue for limitations on sovereignty, given the fact that he had defined sovereignty as unconditional and unrestrained power? Preston King takes the view that when Bodin speaks of sovereignty as absolute, perpetual and total, his claims cannot be squared with his contention that the sovereign is limited by law.[21] There is clearly a problem here. However, it is a problem inherent in the very notion of sovereignty as state power, and it is one which the modernist conception of sovereignty brings sharply to the fore.

As a *modern* thinker, Bodin identified sovereignty with the power of the political community *as a whole* and not (as in premodern conceptions) with this or that component part. On the one hand, sovereignty has to be limited since it cannot be allowed to jeopardize the unity of ruler and ruled. This, indeed, is the link between the modern conception of sovereignty and liberalism, and it pivots on the notion of the individual whose freely expressed consent authorizes the power of the state. At the same time, sovereignty involves unrestricted power since anything less than total power would imply a dualism between ruler and ruled – a fractured community without the capacity to make *new* laws according to an unfettered will. Thus the modernist conception of sovereignty as expounded by Bodin has a logic which embraces limitation and absolutism at the same time.

Both elements are integral to this conception of sovereignty, and it would be wrong to stress one at the expense of the other. Franklin argues that because Bodin was fearful of the anarchy generated by religious disputes in sixteenth-century France, the legal limitations to which he alludes do not (and cannot) formally 'restrain' the sovereign. The prince who violated the limitations placed upon sovereignty is answerable to God, not to the people.[22] Yet despite this, limits are definitionally crucial since the sovereign monarchy (at least in the European context) can only rule through the law, and must therefore accept the restrictions imposed by natural, divine and customary law. The inconsistency here, however, is not peculiar to Bodin. It is rooted (as we shall see) in the entire modernist project.

Absolutism is as important as anti-absolutism. Not only does Bodin allow the lawful sovereign to exercise a power beyond consent, but even the prudential restrictions on sovereignty to which he refers are only relevant to the sovereign in Europe. 'Lordly monarchy', of the kind which Bodin thought prevailed in Asia or among the ancient Egyptians, involved a prince governing his subjects 'as the father of a family governs his slaves'. Sovereignty can embrace lawful as well as overtly tyrannical power, the difference simply being a difference in the mode of (geographically appropriate) governance.[23]

There is an interesting irony here. No pre-modern tyrant would have described sovereignty as unrestrained power since this proposition involves secularizing power in a startlingly modernist way. On the other hand, it has to be said that the modern conception constitutes a refreshingly realistic view of state sovereignty *in all its forms*. The restrictions explicitly built into earlier conceptions of sovereignty are mystical and other-worldly and, accordingly, have to be regarded as theoretical rather than practical in character. They are not to be taken as face value. Roman emperors might *claim* that they derived their absolute power from the people and ruled only with popular consent, but it is clear that they did no such thing.[24]

Bodin makes it possible to identify sovereignty in pre-modern forms even though these are periods in which the conception itself had yet to be explicitly developed. Sovereignty can be said to exist, therefore, even in contexts where it is not conceptualized in consistent terms. Here there is an analogy with the state. The term may be modern, but the reality is traditional. In the same way, the notion of sovereignty as unrestrained power is a modern one, but the reality of sovereignty as a supremacy exercised through hierarchical and repressive institutions is as old as (and indeed an integral part of) the state itself.

In later chapters I will address the problem of formulating a post-statist notion of sovereignty, but here I am concerned to establish that sovereignty in its statist form is not modern. It has existed for about 5000 years. It is certainly true that the modern concept of sovereignty dramatically alters our understanding of the question. By emphasizing the absolutist and unrestrained character of state supremacy, it becomes possible to identify sovereignty in its (admittedly undeveloped and less consistent) pre-modern forms.

Hobbes and the problem of dualism

Hinsley argues that although Bodin's theory of sovereignty was essentially modern, it was incomplete. The notion that political society is limited by divine and natural law leaves the division between ruler and ruled intact, since it assumes that each continues to have 'separate and inextinguishable personalities and rights'. Hobbes, Hinsley tells us, was able to go beyond Bodin by dissolving away the dualism between prince and people. In place of the rights of the community as expressed in customary and natural law, he substituted the 'equal rightlessness of men as individuals before the state that was their own creation'. The authority of the ruler is nothing more than the authority, will and action of every individual.[25]

King comments that whereas Bodin distinguished between sovereign authority and a diminuendo of many other corporate authorities, Hobbes's basic structural distinction was between the sovereign and the subject – the individual and the state. Bodin, King argues, began 'a process of analysis which Hobbes may be said to have completed' – a point which is echoed by Hinsley as well.[26] But the problem of consistency remains. It is true that, for Hobbes, all law (including natural, divine or customary law) derives only from the sovereign. At the same time, Hobbes allows rights against the state – rights which are enjoyed by all individuals equally. The sovereign only exists to provide security and freedom. Sovereignty is therefore restricted to the basic purpose for which individuals have originally covenanted to form a state – the preservation of their lives.

The problem of a power which is both unrestrained and yet limited has not been solved. Rosenberg argues that sovereignty for Hobbes is not directed against the remnants of feudal corporatism (as it is for Bodin), but is concerned with the self-destructive power of individuals in a 'state of nature' – that is, within an incipiently private mode of surplus extraction operating according to the logic of the market.[27] But while this may help to explain why Hobbes's theory is more consistently modernist than Bodin's (and why, Rosenberg argues, realists don't read Bodin), the similarity between the two is striking. Indeed, Rosenberg underlines this similarity when he notes (citing Ellen Wood) that Hobbes basically transplanted Bodin's 'idea of absolute and indivisible sovereignty' to English conditions. The point is that both theorists are modern in that they bring to the fore the problem of a sovereignty which is both limited and (explicitly) absolute.[28]

Rosenberg argues that, for Hobbes, sovereignty is all the 'more absolutist precisely because it was not absolutist'. But this paradox also applies to Bodin even though Bodin's treatment of natural and divine law is more archaic than Hobbes's analysis of the state and the individual. When Rosenberg comments that 'modern sovereignty is only allowed to be so absolute because it involves restricting much more closely what is to count as the legitimate domain of politics',[29] he captures rather aptly the way in which modernity does not resolve, but exposes even more dramatically, the dilemma of state sovereignty.

Modernism and the problematic character of state sovereignty

If we identify sovereignty simply with its modern form, we actually miss what is really startling and critical about modernity. It is only with the rise of the modern state that it becomes possible to *differentiate* what was hitherto conceived in organic unity. But if a differentiated analysis of the state and sovereignty is exhilarating, it also enables us to see just how troubled the concept of state sovereignty really is. The realists in international relations theory are right to see something of universal significance about modernity, but wrong to assume that all sovereign states are basically the same. Rosenberg and Hinsley for their part are right to see the modern state as different, but wrong to assume that because it is different it has nothing in common with its predecessors. A critical view of sovereignty is one which stresses *both* continuity *and* discontinuity in historical analysis. This is why we need to embrace, and at the same time go beyond, the modernist differentiation of state from society.

Both Rosenberg and Hinsley see sovereignty as 'abstract', even if Hinsley does not endorse the connotation of repression and mystification which the concept of 'abstraction' has in Marxist theory. But whether the equation of sovereignty and the modern state is expressed sympathetically[30] or pejoratively, the argument nevertheless remains vulnerable. For the point is that the modern state accentuates and highlights a problem with sovereignty which has existed all along.

The more the autonomy and the impersonality of the state are stressed, the more problematic its sovereignty becomes. On the one hand, sovereignty is seen as universal in its jurisdiction. At the same time, what makes this state sovereignty explicit is the fact that it is public rather than private – that it is *separate* from the society it penetrates. Bhikhu Parekh has argued that the state–society relationship has baffled political theorists for the past four centuries and continues to resist adequate conceptualization.[31] The bafflement is understandable since what is private is apparently determined by what is public, and essential to the particularity of state sovereignty is that it has a hand in everything. This is the reason, as we will see in Chapter 6, why the concept of democracy poses a devastating challenge to sovereignty as a statist concept.

The problem of an unrestrained power which is limited, captures a dilemma inherent in the idea of state sovereignty as a whole. Those who seek to evade this dilemma by emphasizing either the absolutist character or the liberal character of the modernist view of sovereignty (as encapsulated in the classic texts of Bodin and Hobbes) fail to see that *both* are implied. It is, after all, a defining attribute of the state itself that it claims a monopoly of legitimate force, and this means that its power is both limited and unrestrained. Modernism makes it possible to identify a problem with the state in general.

To suggest that sovereignty is peculiar to the 'abstract' state under modernity, merely absolutizes discontinuity in a way which turns a state-centric realism inside out. A critical view of sovereignty requires that we tackle the link between sovereignty and *all* states, and it is the great merit of the modernist thesis that it enables us to see just how problematic this linkage really is.

Legitimacy and Force

The modernist concept of sovereignty provides crucial insight into the question of sovereignty in general since it underlines the unrestrained and absolute power of the state. Just as it brings the question of unqualified supremacy to the fore, so it explicitly links this power with legitimacy, consent, freedom and authority in a way which is historically unprecedented.

Sovereignty, as it is conceived in the modernist tradition, has to be legitimate either because it accords with the law or because it is authorized by individual consent. In stressing legitimacy and supremacy simultaneously, modernism provides us with unrivalled insight into the paradoxical and absurd character of state sovereignty. For the notion of 'legitimate force' as explicitly identified in modernity is, I want to argue, a contradiction in terms. If we want to take legitimacy seriously (as I believe we must), then the idea needs to be linked to the formulation of a post-statist concept of sovereignty.

Hobbes, Rousseau and the problem of dualism

Like Bodin, Hobbes is concerned to show that sovereign power is legitimate. What makes it legitimate is the fact that, in some sense, it is *limited*. In Bodin's case these limits are less modern than they are in Hobbes's; but in the case of both, the point about sovereignty is that it constitutes a 'free people'. A sovereignty not 'limited' to this objective is not sovereignty.

Thus, in Hobbes, the terror of the state has to be legitimated by the 'free will' of the individual. Both elements are critical to his theory. It is true that Rousseau castigates Hobbes in *The Social Contract* for treating humans as cattle, but what makes Rousseau himself one of the classic exponents of modernism is his own insistence upon the unitary and illimitable character of state sovereignty.[1] Where, then, lies the difference between Hobbes and Rousseau?

On this, Hinsley's analysis is most revealing. On the one hand, he cites Otto Gierke to the effect that with Rousseau the history of the doctrine of popular sovereignty comes to an end. If sovereignty implies a unitary body politic in which the division between ruler and ruled has been overcome, then Rousseau seems to have had the last word on the subject. On the other hand, Rousseau's 'solution' to the problem of dualism makes Hinsley understandably nervous. He complains that Rousseau simply reverses Hobbes by allowing the community to swallow up the state.

This is a nervousness which is shared by David Held. Hobbes, Held argues, places the state in an all-powerful position with respect to the community, while Rousseau allows the community to dominate the individual through his concept of the general will. Both project models of political power with potentially tyrannical implications. As Held comments: 'conceptions of sovereignty which fail to demarcate the limits or legitimate scope of political action need to be treated with the utmost caution'.[2]

But it has to be said that Hobbesian and Rousseauian notions of sovereignty *are* limited. Rousseau speaks of people obeying laws which they have prescribed for themselves, and Hobbes argues that the sovereign only exists to enable people to preserve themselves. In both cases sovereignty is limited by the need to maintain (in some sense of the term) individual freedom. If these 'limits' do not seem persuasive but should be expressed in formal constitutional terms (as Held argues), how is this to be done without dividing sovereignty, and thus returning to the dualist notions which the modernist conception of sovereignty (that is, sovereignty in its most consistent statist form) sought to overcome?

Merriam argues that 'Rousseau accomplished for the people what Hobbes had done for the ruler',[3] but the point is that both Hobbes and Rousseau identify sovereignty with the state. It is not that one theorist stresses the community at the expense of the state while the other stresses the state at the expense of the community. On the contrary, as modernists, both Hobbes and Rousseau seek to transcend what Hinsley calls 'the ineradicable distinction between the political community and the state'.

In Hobbes's argument, Merriam says gingerly, the logic is 'cruelly complete' and, granting the necessary premises, the conclusions 'difficult to escape'.[4] But if this is true of Hobbes, it is even more so of Rousseau. The difference between Hobbes and Rousseau is that Hobbes allows individuals a natural right to survival against a sovereign who endangers them, while Rousseau seeks to seal this residual dualism by arguing that individuals are inextricably tied to a 'general will'. In other words, Rousseau offers a solution (albeit a statist one) to the problem of unity between state and society which Hobbes's mechanistic view of the individual prevents him from espousing.

Locke, modernity and the problem of limits

Held's fear of Hobbesian and Rousseauian absolutism leads him to favour a Lockian solution to the problem of state sovereignty. But the problem is that Locke's conception is not consistently modernist in character. Hinsley points out that Locke was loath to discuss the concept of sovereignty 'and never used this word'. It may be that Locke's similarities with Hobbes are more important than their differences,[5] but at the same time Locke demonstrates graphically the problem of trying to reconcile the notion of a constitutionally limited (and thus supposedly legitimate) state with the concept of sovereignty.

Take Locke's celebrated argument that the people can resist a state which tramples upon individual rights. This assumes that sovereignty is divided between the state and people – a point which leads Hinsley to comment that Locke's argument 'retained close affinities with medieval ideas'.[6] On the one hand, Locke allows the commonwealth 'supreme or legislative power'. On the other hand, this supremacy is not sovereign in the modernist sense since it is formally and explicitly limited. Thus the legislature cannot, for example, dispose of the estates of the subject in a way which is considered arbitrary. In other words, sovereignty appears to be *divided*.

A sovereign people can resist a sovereign state. We are back with the dualism of pre-modernist theory, and Hinsley is right to note that Locke reflects the remnants of the belief in a contract between the community and the government – a belief which (in terms of modernist logic) is archaic in character. Joseph Camilleri and Jim Falk see Locke reaffirming the medieval tradition that moral laws are superior to positive law, thereby 'undermining the supremacy of power and authority which Bodin, Hobbes and others had come to regard as the essential ingredient of sovereignty'. But surely, it might be argued, this is a sensible and moderate position to adopt. The state has some sovereignty and so do the people. Merriam argues that with Locke, political society is the latent sovereign which only becomes 'active' when government dissolves.[7]

Indeed, Held even sees Locke as attempting to transcend 'the old dualism' between ruler and people by identifying supreme power as the inalienable right of the people. Governmental supremacy is, Held suggests, a '*delegated* supremacy held on trust'. Locke developed a notion of constitutional government as 'a legal and institutional mechanism to protect both the "sovereign people" and the "sovereign state" – the right of the people to hold political power accountable and the right of the state to govern'.[8]

But this notion of a divided sovereignty is open to the modernist objection that it is not only logically incoherent but also imposes limits of a mystical and implausible kind. If we endorse the existence of the state as an institution which claims a monopoly of legitimate force, then a popular sovereignty enjoyed outside the confines of this state can only be hypothetical in character. Thus ironically it is Hobbes, as Leo Strauss rightly observes, who stresses more strongly than Locke 'the individual's right to resist society or government whenever his self-preservation is threatened'. Who argues that (male) individuals are duty-bound to fight for the state? It is Locke rather than Hobbes.[9]

Locke is a *statist* and, whatever (hypothetical) limits he proposes, the logic of his position points to the supremacy of the state. According to Held (and this is a 'Lockian' argument which Held supports), Hinsley sees the community as the source of sovereignty, and the state as the proper instrument for its exercise. But this is not quite what Hinsley says. Hinsley speaks of the community as 'being wholly *or partly* the source of sovereignty', and the equivocation here is all important. For Hinsley himself concedes that the notion of a 'shared' sovereignty is 'an imperfect solution' to the ancient problem: where does sovereignty lie? This ancient problem can only be settled by what Hinsley calls 'the fluctuating but ever necessary compromise between government and community'.[10]

The difficulty is this. Concepts of shared sovereignty and fluctuating but necessary compromises between the state and community, merely retreat from the logic of modernism. The modernist concept rightly identifies sovereignty as a unitary concept – you either have sovereignty or you don't – but it wrongly identifies sovereignty with the state. Those who are (understandably) alarmed about the limits of a state power which is explicitly characterized as unrestrained in character have a choice. Either they can challenge the very notion of the state, with its problematic claim to exercise a monopoly of legitimate force, or they can return to archaic dualisms which assert limits to state power of an other-worldly and implausible kind.

In other words, no advance beyond the modernist conception is possible as long as we equate sovereignty with the state. The paralysing dualism between state and society (which modernism perfects) is elevated into an organizing principle by Immanuel Kant who sees the theoretical sovereignty of the people simply coexisting with the practical sovereignty of the state. Hinsley argues that it is along this Kantian track that the concept of sovereignty has developed ever since.[11]

Should we segregate the sovereign law from all notions of morality as legal positivists do, and, like Austin and Bentham, revert to a Hobbesian argument shorn of its critical features? Or should we try to tackle the problem of limits by distinguishing between legal and political sovereignty – *de jure* and *de facto* sovereignty – between internal and external sovereignty? All these 'solutions' remain within the framework of the state, and therefore reproduce the dualisms which are inherent in sovereignty as a statist concept.

The problem of force

Over 60 years ago, Francis Coker commented that however divided theorists were over what constituted sovereignty, they could at least agree that the state executes its commands through the 'organized force of the community'.[12] It is this claim to exercise a monopoly of legitimate force which makes states appear sovereign, no matter how alarming and immoral the consequences of this sovereignty might seem.

Force and legitimacy, I want to argue, exclude one another. If legitimacy involves the recognition of limits, force involves their destruction. Hinsley argues that authority, whether it is notional or tangible, is by definition the authority of the state.[13] But why? Why should we assume that sovereignty as an expression of ultimate power is only conceivable in *statist* terms? The equation of sovereignty with the state creates a fundamental problem with legitimacy.

In Hobbes's theory, both force and freedom receive equal emphasis. Force is both tied to legitimacy and defined in a way which excludes it. Thus, in Hobbes's view, no person can surrender the right to resist those 'that assault him by force' – 'a Covenant not to defend my selfe from force, by force, is always voyd'.[14] Rousseau is troubled with the same problem. He declares in impeccably liberal fashion that 'force is a physical power; I do not see how its effects could produce morality', while he famously argues the case for forcing people to be free. And force, despite what some have argued, means force.[15] Penalties up to and including execution, for example, are to be imposed upon those who express disbelief in a civil religion.

States can take many different forms, but in all of them, as D'Entreves comments, 'force has to be resorted to' and 'force has to be effective'. Attempts to suggest that force is compatible with legitimacy are not, in my view, persuasive. Rodney Barker has argued that the state is legitimate for the privileged and powerful, but not legitimate for the weak and oppressed.[16] However, this argument simply side-steps rather than resolves the problem raised by Hobbes and Rousseau. If all states necessarily claim a monopoly of legitimate force, then the problem arises: how can one consent to this use of force? David Beetham is right to insist that legitimacy must be conceived as a *relationship* between parties bound together by shared beliefs and by some kind of common interest. These commonalities constitute the defining limits to a relationship, and are thus crucial to its legitimacy. In Beetham's view, a relationship may be oppressive and still be legitimate, as in the case, say, of a paternalistic exercise of power in which children or women or slaves accept as 'natural' and unproblematic their subordinate status.[17]

While all this is plausible, it does not make the case for reconciling legitimacy with force. For if legitimacy requires a relational acceptance of common values by both parties, force disrupts this commonalty since force necessarily involves treating subjects as objects and people as things. The use of force cannot be subject to that mutual recognition of limits that is the defining attribute of a relationship. Beetham argues that force is legitimate when it is used to protect citizens.[18] But although it is true that in a particular situation the only way to secure protection against a bully, thug or terrorist, say, may be through the defensive use of force, force is still incompatible with legitimacy.

Using force against force (however provisionally) places us in the hapless position of having to undermine freedom in order to secure it. In other words, we may have to sacrifice legitimacy in the short term in order to provide relief from those who would otherwise inflict force upon us. But the illegitimate character of force remains all the same. For the point is that force is not simply illegitimate for the recipient who is degraded and harmed through force (if he or she is not immediately extinguished). Force is also illegitimate for the administrator or perpetrator. To treat a person as a thing is to dehumanize oneself in the process. When force is employed – by the state or in response to the state – legitimacy is undermined, and this is why Rousseau frankly acknowledges that his attempt to establish a 'legitimate' state necessarily fails.[19]

It is no use trying to get round this problem by arguing that sovereignty is irrelevant to the daily life of the 'normal' state. Crick pleads for a 'real distinction' between what he calls the time of sovereignty and the time of politics, but his problem is this. He identifies both politics and sovereignty with the state, so that small groups, for example, cannot be political, because 'unlike the state, they have no acknowledged legal right to use force if all else fails'.[20] It is precisely this right to use force 'if all else fails' which creates the problem, and here Crick equivocates. On the one hand, he defines politics as an activity 'which chooses conciliation rather than violence and coercion'. On the other hand, he identifies politics as 'a way of ruling divided societies without undue violence'.[21] But however free and conciliatory politics is supposed to be, Crick insists that at the end of the day it involves force.

It is not difficult to see that force inevitably brings conciliation to an abrupt halt since it involves imposing on individuals, solutions which are explicitly against their will. Moreover, as I have noted above, the exercise of force does not simply undermine legitimacy or freedom for a few. The force of the state is, in Rousseau's words, 'collective' in character. It cannot but compromise the existence of legitimacy for *all* the members of a state-centred society.

Force and the stateless society

Political theorists have generally embraced what I want to call the
Hobbesian assumption, namely that without the organized force of
the state, order and civilization are impossible. Government
requires force, and sovereignty without force is inconceivable.
While King argues quite rightly that the need for order arises from
the fact that each individual 'impinges' upon another, he is wrong
to insist that every governmental order 'at some point sanctions the
use of violence'.[22] For this argument equates government with the
state, and assumes that without the use of force, order would be
impossible.

The question is this: why should we assume that government as
a process of settling disputes, can only take place through an institution which claims a monopoly of legitimate force? Easton rightly
argues that the notion that government must by definition involve
the use of force is an ethnocentric one. It is important to remind
ourselves that humankind has conducted its affairs for most of its
existence without a state, and anthropologists in the post-war
period have shown in detail how this is possible. Government is a
process of resolving conflicts of interest. It should be distinguished
from the activity of the state.[23]

Hinsley is most revealing on this. His definition of sovereignty is
a statist one. It is only through the state, he argues, that it is possible to identify a final and absolute political authority in the community. However, he also comments that in a stateless society there
is no single central symbol of rule, whereas 'a single headship is the
mark for the presence of the state'. The notion of sovereignty as a
statist *oneness* is quintessentially Hobbesian in character, and, as
Hinsley acknowledges, oneness implies force.[24] In stateless
societies, disputes cannot be settled through force since 'there is a
balance of opposed local loyalties and ritual ties'.

This point is confirmed in Clastres's study of the Amerindians.
The chief, Clastres argues, who sought to issue a command backed
by sanctions of physical force, would be met by certain refusal and
a denial of further recognition. In what Clastres calls 'society
against the state', sovereignty as a notion of concentrated force
does not exist.[25] It is important that we do not idealize the governmental mechanisms of these early societies. Not only do (or
did) these societies encompass tiny and culturally homogenous

populations living with subsistence economies, but they were (at least in some cases) not free from violence. In today's world, with our modern technology, we would be right to regard spontaneous outbreaks of violence of the kind that manifested themselves in some early stateless societies as menacing and unacceptable.

Nevertheless, what such societies *do* provide is a crucial insight into the way in which order can be secured without the state. As Hinsley comments, 'the notion of defeat is normally absent. The weaker of two segments will retreat rather than fight, and if one segment does defeat another it does not attempt to establish dominance over it.' This is a point which Mair underlines in her study of the Nuer in Sudan. Even when outbreaks of violence do occur, she argues, this force is not used 'as a means of dominating others'. Orderly relations within the community are secured without and *despite* the use of force.[26]

Among the New Jale of Guinea, fighting, as Simon Roberts notes, is highly ritualized so as to minimize disruption to the normal life of the community. In the case of the native American tribes that Clastres studied, an outbreak of violence would represent a *failure* of government which could only undermine the prestige of the chief. This notion of government without the state is also crucial in understanding how order is possible *between* states in a world which is itself 'anarchical' or stateless in character. We need, therefore, to distinguish between *conflict* which implies a dispersal of activity among multiple actors, and *force* which (when employed in a statist fashion) requires domination.[27]

Force as a mechanism of domination is used either by the state or against the state. It is the distinguishing feature of the state that it responds to force in a forceful way. It has been argued by Stanley Johnson that violence differs from force in that the former violates some moral or legal norm, whereas the latter does not. But such a distinction is untenable. While it may be true (as I have noted above) that state force is inevitable in situations in which conflicts of interest cannot be 'contained' in any other way, this force still involves violence – that is, it *violates* the freedom and subjectivity of the individual or group against whom it is directed.[28] The point is that force (or violence) as a method of resolving conflicts of interest is specific to state-centred societies. It cannot be reconciled with legitimacy.

Force, coercion and the problem of community

State sovereignty, I have argued, has a built-in legitimacy problem. But how are stateless societies to govern if they have no institution which claims a monopoly of legitimate force?

Again on this matter Hinsley is revealing. 'In a stateless society', he comments, 'authority relies on psychological and moral coercion rather than on force', and this is a crucial point. Government in stateless societies involves negotiation, discussion and compromise.[29] Where punishments have to be meted out and rules enforced, the sanctions employed in stateless societies involve pressures which cannot be described as force. As Easton comments, any attempt to equate moral coercion with physical force would mean divesting the latter of its meaning.[30] The distinction between force and coercion is crucial to understanding how we can achieve order without the state.

Of course coercion takes many forms. To speak (as we often do) of coercion as the *threat* to use force makes the distinction between them wafer-thin. But it is a distinction none the less worth preserving. For, strictly speaking, coercion is simply a 'pressure' which causes individuals to act in ways which they would otherwise have avoided. The point about force is that it prevents people from acting at all. Coercion can be quite diffuse in form, as in the case of what John Stuart Mill calls 'natural penalties'. These arise simply because we live in society and therefore everything we do affects the activities of everyone else. Hence, I would argue that coercion *of some kind* is inherent in society, and is a precondition of, rather than a hindrance to, our freedom.[31]

Even in its more 'concentrated' forms, coercion falls short of force. It is true that recalcitrant parties may need to be 'bullied' or 'cajoled' into accepting settlements, and early societies resorted to shaming and ostracism, ridicule and even supernatural sanctions in securing order. However unpleasant coercion might be (and in particular cases even indefensible), it is nevertheless qualitatively different from force. In and of itself coercion does not prevent an individual from exercising choice. Force does. This is why legitimacy (which involves the recognition of limits) is compatible with coercion, even though, as we have seen, it is necessarily undermined by force.

Hinsley comments that whenever the state has been successfully established, 'we shall find a conflict between the principle of community and the principle of dominance'.[32] I agree. The very existence of the state signals the fact that the community can no longer settle conflict in ways which respect the identity of all the parties to a dispute. In contrasting the mechanisms for securing order in a stateless with those of a state-centred society, Hinsley provides the conceptual tools (even if he does not employ them himself) for demonstrating the problematic character of state sovereignty. For if state sovereignty involves, as I have argued, the imposition of force ('the principle of domination') as a way of resolving conflicts of interest, then we have an institution which is inherently divisive and contradictory in character.

Where the state exists, sections of a fractured community necessarily challenge its professed monopoly by resorting to an unauthorized force of their own. In this way, they contest the legitimacy of the state they resist. Of course, such individuals or groups are invariably characterized in official discourse as 'impossible' minorities whose resort to force seems inexplicably horrendous to all right-thinking people. But the point is that these individuals or groups are there all the same. Their presence signals the fact that the community in whose name state sovereignty is exercised does not actually exist.

We can, in my view, take it for granted that the state's claim to exercise a monopoly of legitimate force is necessarily rejected by those against whom it is targeted. States embody in their very structures the kind of division which undermines legitimacy, and if we fail to challenge states, they will conceptually paralyse all attempts to offer a coherent definition of sovereignty.

Democracy

I have argued that what makes sovereignty impossibly contentious as a concept is its relationship to the state. Democracy is, in my view, a concept whose logic points to self-government. Its collision with sovereignty only makes sense when sovereignty itself is interpreted in statist terms.

If notions of popular sovereignty are problematic, this is not because they are democratic but rather, I want to argue, because they are frequently *statist* in character. An argument for a cosmopolitan democracy – a democracy for the world as a whole – is only coherent when it analyses democracy as a method of settling conflicts of interests which goes beyond the state.

Democracy and the state

Democracy is frequently pitted against sovereignty. But the democratic critique of sovereignty is only tenable when it tackles the reality of the state. To attack sovereignty in the name of democracy while leaving the conceptual premises of the state unscathed, leads to the notion of a shared or divided sovereignty which modernist conceptions have rightly ridiculed and sought to overcome.

This problem is apparent in Maritain's blistering attack on sovereignty which Camilleri and Falk cite with approval. Maritain presents sovereignty as an absolutist concept which points to the existence of a power above, and separate from, the body politic. Defined thus, sovereignty undermines any notion of popular rule since it would be nonsensical to imagine the government of the people taking place 'separately from themselves and above themselves'. Sovereignty is incompatible with democracy.[1] However, because Maritain identifies sovereignty simply with its modernist formulation, he offers an uncritical view of the state itself. The state, he argues, is not and has never been sovereign. Its 'supreme independence and power' are subject to the laws and administration of the body politic. As far as Maritain is concerned, the right of the people to govern themselves is limited by a natural law which derives from the sovereignty of God.[2]

Stankiewicz notes that Maritain takes it for granted that democracy is a form of the state. But if this is so, Stankiewicz protests, popular self-government is a contradiction in terms. It is absurd 'to talk of anyone governing himself or any group ruling itself, for there cannot then be any "government"'. This is an old argument indeed. Define government in terms of the *state*, and we are confronted by a cleavage between ruler and ruled which makes it impossible for people to govern themselves.[3]

Stankiewicz does, however, concede that if we define democracy in post-statist terms, the 'right to self-government' is indeed 'incompatible with the theory of sovereignty'. As a 'fact of political life', sovereignty 'is inconveniently at odds with democratic assumptions of what ought to be'. Stankiewicz takes the view that in the 'real world' 'no democratic society has been characterized by true self-government'. At the same time, he acknowledges that as a concept, democracy seems to lend itself to 'hypothetical' and 'purist' formulations, and so he concedes cautiously: 'Perhaps a complete reconciliation [between sovereignty and democracy] is not possible here'. When the need for action in the face of an implicit threat of conflict arises (that is, when institutionalized force has to be used), 'the logic of sovereignty prevails over the logic of democracy'.[4]

While Stankiewicz is right to dismiss Maritain's statist challenge to the concept of sovereignty, he is conscious that there is a real problem here. Democracy as a 'logic' points beyond the state. This is also the celebrated point which Plato makes in *The Republic* when he attacks democracy as a system which turns 'natural' hierarchies upside down. Fathers and sons, he protests, change places and 'there's no distinction between citizens, alien and foreigner'. Slaves come to enjoy the same freedom as their owners, not to mention the complete equality and liberty in the relations between the sexes. Such is the extremism of democracy that in the end even domestic animals are infected with anarchy![5]

Although it has to be said that ancient Greek supporters of democracy interpreted the latter in a statist fashion, Plato, like Aristotle, champions the state against democracy. Aristotle argues that the state itself 'belongs to a class of objects which exist in nature', and this is why he assumes that in all political systems the question will inevitably arise: where does 'sovereign power' (that is, statist supremacy) lie?[6] The point about democracy is this. It has an egalitarian 'logic' which is incompatible with notions of state supremacy, whether these are presented in a modernist or archaic way.

The question of federalism

It is argued that because federalism is essential to democracy, it is a challenge to the concept of sovereignty. Thus when, in 1917, Harold Laski extols the merits of federalism in the USA, he does so as part of his critique of state sovereignty. A federalist democracy, he argues, is at war with sovereignty because checks and balances prevent monopolistic concentrations of power, and 'we do not know who rules'. Neither the president, nor Congress nor the Supreme Court, can be said to be absolute, Laski enthuses, while 'certain sovereign rights' are possessed by the states alone.

This argument was later repeated by Robert Dahl in the case he makes for pluralist democracy in his classic *Who Governs?* It rests upon the assumption that, if we take the USA with its federalist constitution as 'the shape of democracy itself' as Tocqueville did,[7] then federalism appears as the antithesis of state sovereignty. No one denies that the USA is federalist. But is it not also true to say that its political system centres around an institution claiming a monopoly of legitimate force? Harold Laski was later to argue that it is the 'coercive authority' of the state which makes it sovereign, and this point rather complicates his earlier contrast between federalism and state sovereignty. The USA, he concedes, is a state (however federalist) whose sovereignty is vested in its constitution, and those who control the use of the armed forces of this state are the masters of its sovereignty. This a point on which Crick concurs. The granting of military power to the American presidency, he comments, is no more and no less than what Hobbes meant in his famous aphorism 'covenants without the sword are vain'.[8]

It is still possible, through a narrow and exclusively modernist view of sovereignty, to argue (as Hinsley does) that federalist states are not sovereign. But this is misleading. As King has commented, federal institutions can only be said to overthrow the traditional theory of sovereignty (as he calls it) if it can be demonstrated that more than one ultimate power exists within a single state. In fact, as pluralists themselves acknowledge, all federal governments (that is, states) implicitly or explicitly exclude the right of their component parts to secede.[9] The point, then, is that despite their distinctive characteristics, federalist systems are still sovereign states. They cannot overcome (whatever their champions believe) the tension which exists between democracy as self-government and an institution which claims to exercise a monopoly of legitimate force.

The problem of popular sovereignty

Camilleri and Falk speak of a 'widening gap' between state sovereignty and popular sovereignty. This gap, they argue, reflects the state's growing separation from civil society. Popular sovereignty is linked to related notions such as pluralism, autonomy, freedom and accountability. At the heart of this conceptual cluster lies democracy.[10]

This argument is central to Daniel Deudney's recent critique of what he calls the Westphalian model of sovereignty – the model which has characterized the European state system since the Treaty of Westphalia in the seventeenth century. Deudney contends that while this model enshrined the concept of state sovereignty expounded by Bodin and Hobbes, an alternative system of sovereignty can be found in (what he calls) the Philadelphian system. This operated in the USA between the establishment of Union and the outbreak of the Civil War (1861–5). It embodied a sovereignty which was not statist, but which, in James Madison's words, derived from the 'ultimate authority' of the people.[11]

In the Philadelphian model, Deudney argues, all actors were 'constitutive members of the sovereign'. There was no hierarchy in which some ruled over others, and actual governance was carried out by authorities delegated with power on behalf of 'a recessed sovereign public'.[12] But the problem with this notion of sovereignty is that, despite its supposedly popular character, it still allows a role for ultimate *force*. Echoing Hobbes's admonition that covenants need swords, Deudney comments that 'the founders sought to guarantee that the sword would remain firmly in the hands of the sovereign, the people'. Both within and between member states, statist sovereignty operated.

Within each state, as Deudney makes clear, order was construed in terms of a political economy of 'possessive individualism', and this meant in practice that supposedly democratic systems embraced patriarchy, the dispossession of native Americans, disfranchisement for 'dependants' and, in the case of some states, outright slavery. Between the states, military autonomy was explicitly circumscribed. Overall power was vested in a union-wide state which had the president as commander-in-chief, while a central government was empowered to raise and support a standing army and navy.[13] Deudney acknowledges that once the USA was torn apart by civil war, both parties to the dispute resorted to the Westphalian notion of sovereignty. Southerners argued that the people of each member state had the ultimate right to secede, while the North located sovereignty in the unionist state of a majoritarian nation. Both moved away from the distinctive Philadelphian model which had vested sovereignty in the people as a whole.

We are willing to accept that this Philadelphian model of sovereignty has features which differentiate it from the Westphalian. But the point is surely that it is naive to regard the Philadelphian system as a model of popular *rather than* state sovereignty, since the principle of statist rule still operated (albeit in a distinctive way) at both local and federal level. Deudney argues that 'to constitute themselves as a sovereign, the people of the United States had to assume and sustain a particular political community and identity'.[14] But this is precisely the point. When we examine the 'particularity' of this 'community and identity', it becomes clear why sovereignty in the Philadelphian model took a statist and therefore a divisive and exclusive form.

It has been estimated that when the Declaration of Independence was proclaimed in 1776, there were some 650,000 slaves, 250,000 indentured servants and 300,000 Indians – roughly 40 per cent of the adult male population. In addition, of course, women had no vote. Deudney concedes that republicanism in the USA centred on 'free soil, free men',[15] but he fails to see why the notion of popular sovereignty he expounds has a treacherously ideological content.

Tocqueville's *Democracy in America* is famous for its celebration of popular sovereignty in the USA. But there is an extraordinary tension in Tocqueville's argument between his notion of democracy as embodying an egalitarian political logic, and his portrait of a society rooted in property ownership. On the one hand, he argues (in almost Platonic terms) that democracy is a 'universal and permanent' force for equality. Having destroyed feudalism and vanquished kings, it will not 'fall back before the middle class and the rich'. At the same time, he identifies property ownership as the secret of America's success, and comments that maxims called democratic in France would be outlawed in the United States.[16]

The point is that the property ownership which Tocqueville explored was exclusive in character. It is true that Philadelphian America lacked a class of proletarians in the European sense, and Tocqueville was struck by just how relatively widespread the ownership of property (usually land) was. But if there were no European-style proletarians in the 1830s, there *were* dispossessed native Americans and enslaved blacks whose plunder and exploitation was hardly incidental to the fact that property was owned by most of the adult white males.[17] To speak of democracy as popular sovereignty in this context is rendered problematic by the existence of a state which sought to impose order upon (among others) those women, blacks and native Americans who were explicitly excluded from the ranks of the 'people'.

Tocqueville's searing critique of the racism, genocide, fraud and plunder to which 'Indians' and blacks were subject by the colonists still repays reading today. It is true that Tocqueville speaks of native Americans and blacks as 'tangents to my subject', but it could well be argued that his own scathing denunciation of America's policy of genocide and enslavement places a question mark over his characterization of the USA as an 'immense and complete democracy'.[18] If democracy involves self-government and popular rule (and Tocqueville himself suggests that its *logic* points in this direction), how is it compatible with the brutalities and divisiveness he so memorably recalls? As long as popular sovereignty takes a statist character, its democratic credentials are in doubt.

Democracy and the tyranny thesis

Dahl argues (rightly, in my view) that when individuals are forced to comply with laws, democracy is to that extent compromised. The very resort to force *undermines* self-government.[19] This point is central to an assessment of those who see democracy and popular sovereignty as politically menacing principles.

At the heart of Crick's critique of democracy is his argument that popular sovereignty is tyrannical in character. The idea that the people constitute a homogeneous totality with a single political will, is sinister and disturbing, since it implies that violence and terror are 'needed to produce unanimity'. The democratic doctrine of the sovereignty of the people threatens the 'essential perception that all known advanced societies are inherently pluralistic and diverse, which is the seed and root of politics'.[20] But Crick's own examples of 'popular tyranny' make it clear that it is the capacity to impose order through force which is the root of the problem.

Chantal Mouffe has argued recently that the logic of democracy and liberalism are ultimately incompatible. Democracy embodies the logic of what she calls identity or equivalence, while liberalism expresses the logic of pluralism or difference. This leads Mouffe to protest that democracy fosters the dictatorial rule of a sovereign popular will.[21] At the same time, she supports a polity which respects difference, diversity and individual self-determination. But is this polity a form of the state? Mouffe's lack of clarity on this issue is exemplified by her attitude towards the pre-war conservative, Carl Schmitt. She admires Schmitt's emphasis on the specificity of politics as the differentiation between friend and foe, and she contrasts this with the tendency by liberal thinkers such as Rawls and Dworkin to 'reduce' (as she puts it) politics to morality, rationality or, in the case of Hayek, the mechanism of the market. But while Schmitt is praised for identifying politics with *conflict*, Mouffe is embarrassed by the fact that Schmitt interprets conflict in an avowedly statist manner.[22]

His reference to the 'elimination' of the enemy should not, she argues, be understood as physical elimination. While she identifies politics with power, conflict and division, she is (understandably) reluctant to endorse Schmitt's classically statist belief that differentiating between friends and foes involves repression and force.[23] If democracy is a form of the state, then Schmitt is right. Democracy does rest upon an oppressive 'logic of identity'. If, on the other hand, democracy is governmental rather than statist (in my terminology), then conflicts can only be resolved in a way which respects the physical integrity of the participants to a dispute.

This is indeed what Mouffe appears to have in mind. She talks of the need to distinguish between the 'social agent' (presumably the physical individual or individuals) and the multiplicity of 'subject positions' which agents precariously and temporarily adopt. But the pluralism of multiple identities which is 'constitutive of modern democracy' and which 'precludes any dream of final reconciliation',[24] only really makes sense if we *detach* democracy from the state. It is the failure to do this that lies at the heart of Mouffe's conceptual confusion and uncertainty.

Those who support the tyranny thesis are unable to see that what makes the idea of popular sovereignty problematic is not that it is democratic, but the fact that it can be construed in a statist fashion. It is the state rather than democracy which undermines the capacity of individuals to settle their differences through conciliation and to enjoy pluralistic and diverse identities.

Democracy and cosmopolitanism

Held has argued that the question of democracy must be theorized in relation to what he calls 'overlapping local, national, regional and global structures and processes'.[25] A cosmopolitan model of democracy is one which engages the realities of the emerging global system.

I have argued elsewhere that Held's model is underpinned by a 'post-statal' logic.[26] Yet this logic is frustrated by an unwillingness to conceptualize sovereignty in a post-statist manner. Held takes the view that the modern state will be with us for the foreseeable future, and that sovereignty needs to be defined in statist terms. Thus, when supranational agencies curtail decision-making within a national framework, sovereignty, he contends, 'is eroded'. Held talks of sovereignty being 'divided' among regional, national and local agencies, and 'limited' by plural institutions.[27]

But this raises the problem already noted in the discussion on legitimacy. If we argue that sovereignty is divided and limited, do we not return to pre-modern concepts of state sovereignty? The challenge which Held poses is this: how are we to *redefine* sovereignty so that it is compatible with plurality, diversity and heterogeneity? Sovereignty, he contends, derives its legitimacy from a cosmopolitan democratic law which embraces subnational entities and transnational communities as well as states. Sovereignty should be stripped away from the idea of fixed borders or territories. As 'malleable time-space clusters', sovereignty manifests itself in diverse self-regulating associations ranging from states to cities and corporations. Held wants to broaden the concept of sovereignty without rejecting the need for a statist definition. However, if democracy involves multiple sites of power, then the monopolistic and absolutist aspirations of the state must be directly confronted. Sovereignty embraces pluralist and multi-layered associations, not because it is divided or shared, but because it needs to be reconceptualized as the attribute of self-regulating entities.[28]

Held is unwilling to detach sovereignty from the state. He insists that the modern state is not defunct but rather that 'its idea' must be adapted 'to stretch across borders'.[29] But this raises the question: what exactly is the state? If we adopt, and I have argued we should, the Weberian view of the state as an institution claiming a monopoly of legitimate force, then democratizing the state involves moving beyond it. This does not mean that the state suddenly disappears in some kind of miraculous puff of smoke. What it means is that under the pressure to democratize, states yield up their distinctive prerogatives. A state which shares power explicitly with other associations is ceasing to be a state.

Held, however, defines the modern state as an 'artificial person' – that is, impersonal power – and argues that this is the principle which can be stretched across borders. But the problem is that Held also accepts that states are institutions which claim a monopoly of force. Thus when he argues for the use of force as a weapon of last resort 'in the face of clear attacks to eradicate cosmopolitan democratic law', he suggests that this force could be provided by nation states seconding a proportion of their military might to international authorities.

While all organizations should aspire to notions of fairness and impartiality associated with the idea of impersonal power, what *differentiates* the state from these organizations is its claim to exercise a monopoly of legitimate force. *Logically*, Held looks beyond the state when he outlines his model of a cosmopolitan democracy. He defends 'the principle of non-coercive relations' (I would prefer to say 'non-violent') in the settlement of disputes and speaks of 'the ultimate aim of demilitarization and the transcendence of the war system'.[30] At the same time, he is reluctant to define sovereignty in a way which challenges the centrality and *raison d'être* of the state.

Democracy and statist discourse

Held himself points to the conceptual tension between democracy and the state. Democratic processes, he argues, depend upon a framework in which non-violent forms of disagreement and conflict resolution can occur – a framework in which all citizens enjoy an equal entitlement to self-determination. If, as Held contends, violence is 'incompatible with democratic forms of decision-making',[31] then that surely represents a challenge to the state and the kind of sovereignty it claims to exercise.

We come to the heart of Held's conceptual problems. He defines sovereignty as the power of self-regulating associations. At the same time, he also retains the atomistic focus of the liberal tradition which leads him to argue that sovereignty, freedom and autonomy must be 'limited' by the constraints of community. The *demos* must rule, Held argues, but within a context which limits 'the scope of popular rule and the reach of popular sovereignty'.[32] But these limitations only arise when we assume that people are statist-minded individuals who will use their freedom, autonomy and sovereignty in antisocial ways unless curbed from on high – by the state!

The *demos*, Held argues, should include all adults 'with the exception of those temporarily visiting a political community, and those who "beyond a shadow of doubt" were legitimately disqualified from participation due to severe mental incapacity and/or serious records of crime'. This assumes that crime and severe mental incapacity are self-evident and natural (that is, there is nothing that anyone can do about them), and that, moreover, they do not interfere with legitimacy and the general conditions of 'equal involvement'.[33] Freedom and autonomy are atomistically conceived – some can enjoy them while others do not. I have already conceded that there is a *tactical* argument for the continuing use of force in situations where common interests have yet to be cemented. But *conceptually* it remains true nevertheless that force undermines freedom and autonomy, and that the exclusion of some from the sovereign right to self-government cannot but undermine the sovereignty of all.

At one point Held argues that democrats should aim to reduce all conditions and institutions which undermine autonomy. However, he characterizes this as an 'ideal' and argues that it should be distinguished from the levels of autonomy which are actually 'attainable'. This point is a problematic one, for it suggests that in practice ideals hang lifelessly outside a dynamic reality[34] – a paralysing dualism for which the sovereign state is to blame. I say this because the sovereign state, even in its most developed liberal form, can do no more than present an idealized view of self-determination which collapses coercion with force, and expounds freedom and autonomy in abstract and atomized terms. An uncritical view of this sovereign state leaves us (like Kant) powerless to resolve the tragic and unbridgeable gulf between ideals and reality.

Held senses a tension between democracy as self-government and the state as an institution claiming a monopoly of legitimate force. But he lacks the conceptual resources to redefine sovereignty in post-statist terms so that its illimitable and indivisible character is located in a world in which individuals, associations, nations and transnational agencies all contribute towards that exercise of autonomy which is central to the democratic process. In a revealing footnote Held accepts that he uses the term 'politics' in two conflicting ways. On the one hand, politics is defined in terms of the state; on the other hand it relates to the capacity of social agents to transform their environment.[35]

Here, in a nutshell, is the equivocation which lies at the heart of Held's analysis of democracy, sovereignty and the state. For if politics involves the state with its claim to a monopoly of force, then what happens to the freedom of individuals as they seek to govern their own lives? If democracy is to become compatible with sovereignty, sovereignty needs to be freed from the monopolistic embraces of the state in a way which is much more consistent and sustained than Held's cosmopolitan model allows.

Feminism

It is widely acknowledged that feminism takes many different forms. The question inevitably arises: is there a feminist position on sovereignty at all? Feminism, I shall argue, is characterized by an emancipatory logic which necessarily challenges the hierarchical divisiveness of the sovereign state.

The feminist critique provides important insights into the state's exclusive character, and some feminists have constructed a notion of self-sovereignty which is central to the task of reclaiming the concept itself. Before examining the contribution which feminist theory makes to the analysis of sovereignty, I need to tackle the question of its heterogeneous identity.

The diversity problem

So diverse has feminism become that even the criteria distinguishing one 'variety' from another are contested. Should we differentiate feminisms along an 'ideological' spectrum, or should the divisions be construed in 'philosophical' terms? Karen Offen distinguishes between dualistic distinctions ('first wave'/'second wave'; 'classical'/'modern'; 'humanistic'/'gynocentric' feminism) and tripartite distinctions ('egalitarian'/'evangelical'/'socialist' as opposed to 'liberal'/'Marxist'/'radical' feminism). Maggie Humm refuses to speak of 'feminism' in the singular in order to stress the concept's diverse and multiple character.

Yet Offen is surely right to argue that we need to arrive at some understanding of the term which we can all agree on.[1] In my view feminism, however diverse, is united by its concern with the

freedom and autonomy of women. This broad definition enables us
to assess the particular contribution which each strand makes to the
emancipation of women as a whole – a process which is integral to
emancipation in general. It is true that feminists such as Mary
Wollstonecraft do not explicitly raise the question of women's
political rights. At the same time, her attack on the 'divine right' of
husbands, her critique of Rousseau's naturalism, and her argument
that women are capable of rationality and autonomy contribute sig-
nificantly to what I have called the emancipatory logic of feminism.

Mill and Taylor do argue for women's suffrage but they embrace
an uncritical view of the sexual division of labour in the family. If
it is true (as Zillah Eisenstein has urged) that all feminism is liberal
at root, the point is that feminism necessarily challenges the patriarchal bias of the liberal tradition.[2] Feminists question (if only
implicitly) the assumption that individuals are property-owning
men, and hence the notion of a 'liberal feminism' is problematic.
Feminism embodies an emancipatory logic, however inconsistent
or incoherent the premises which particular theorists adopt.

The same is true of the concept of a 'socialist or Marxist feminism'. In so far as socialists substitute the community for the individual, they ignore the position of large numbers of women, and so
arguably are not really feminists at all. Marxists who adopt patriarchal notions of production, communism, sexuality and violence
betray anti-feminist prejudices.[3] This is not to deny that particular
socialists or Marxists have contributed to feminist theory. It is
merely to argue that feminism as a theory of female emancipation
remains distinct from the various bodies of thought upon which it
draws.

A similar objection can be raised against 'philosophical' distinctions between feminist empiricism, feminist standpoint theory and
feminist postmodernism.[4] Feminist empiricism, we are told, exam-
ines the 'empirical' ways in which domestic, national and international politics impinge upon women's lives, but it does so as part
of the feminist critique as a whole. Facts help to illuminate patriarchal structures of power so that feminism in general is weakened if
the 'facts' which underpin its critique of patriarchy are segregated
into a separate 'variant'.

The same is true of what has been called feminist standpoint
theory. This assesses the position of women from the 'standpoint'
of those excluded from power. 'On its own' a feminism such as this

is prone to see women as inherently compassionate and caring, and thus tends, as Kathleen Jones has argued, to biologist or naturalistic analyses of women's experience. But the standpoint of women should not be looked at in an abstract and timeless way. Moreover, to take a third 'variant', feminist postmodernism warns of the danger of presenting the experience of particular women as a timeless norm, and assuming that gender should be given a privileged place when analysing the 'binary' exclusion of others.[5]

But here again, one 'variant' should not be isolated from others. Divorce feminist postmodernism from the emancipatory logic of feminism as a whole, and you end up with arguments which, in the name of 'diversity', deny the reality of women as a distinct group. Feminism becomes a theory which abolishes its own constituents, a kind of relativism which has been well described as 'the last ditch stand of modern patriarchy'.[6] Taken in isolation from feminism in general, postmodernist feminism, like standpoint and empiricist feminism, cannot really be called feminist at all. The distinction which is sometimes drawn between feminist postmodernism and postmodern feminism is yet another exercise in divisive abstraction. Proliferating distinctions between this or that 'variant' run the risk of undermining the emancipatory logic of the project as a whole. What unifies feminism, as Offen stresses, is its opposition to women's subordination to men: 'to be a feminist is necessarily to be at odds with male-dominated culture and society'.[7]

This logic of emancipation can only be sustained if it is 'infinite' in character. As Anna Yeatman comments, a feminist politics of emancipation must break with abstract reason and a millenarian notion of finality.[8] A coherent feminism is one, it seems to me, which endorses just such a historically sensitive notion of emancipation.

Feminism and the state

As a theory rooted in a logic of emancipation, feminism looks implicitly beyond the state. However, it has to be said that many feminists do not see the state in this way.

In Heidi Hernes's view, feminist critiques of the state represent a naive anarchism which contrasts with what she calls 'a woman-friendly state'. Zillah Eisenstein concurs. The state itself is not the problem, and she argues the case for 'an affirmative and non-interventionist state' that is pluralist and post-patriarchal in character.[9] Indeed, Judith Allen even contends that the state does not belong to the categories which are relevant for developing feminist theory such as 'law', 'bureaucratic culture', 'the body', 'subjectivity', 'power', 'paternalism' and 'misogyny'. Arguments like these make it impossible to develop a feminist critique of state sovereignty.

Allen protests that while Catherine MacKinnon characterizes the state as male, MacKinnon identifies popular culture, economics, religion, language, football and indeed knowledge in general as male as well. In this way she undermines the specificity of the 'male state' at the very moment that she urges it.[10] This is a good point. Unless we can show that the state is *specifically* patriarchal, then Allen is right. A feminist critique of sovereignty is 'unnecessary'. The problem with MacKinnon is that she argues that because male violence pervades society as a whole, the state is merely one patriarchal institution among many. This ignores the fact that state sovereignty seeks to impose its 'legitimate force' upon *all* who live in a particular society, and it asserts, *inter alia*, the right to probe (in MacKinnon's words) into the home, the bedroom, the job and the street.[11] That male power has this socially pervasive character stems from the patriarchal nature of state sovereignty itself.

Allen accepts that 'violence' is one of the categories which is 'indigenous' (as she puts it) to feminist theory, but it is precisely the use of force as a mechanism for resolving conflicts of interest which characterizes the state. It is revealing that MacKinnon accepts Dahl's view of politics as a system which involves power, authority, coercion and force[12] – a definition that undermines any attempt to distinguish between conflicts which are settled without force, and conflicts which are dealt with by the state. There is no space in MacKinnon's argument for an analysis of conflict resolution in stateless societies. Yet Gerda Lerner has demonstrated in detail how the 'creation' of patriarchy is made possible by the birth of the state. The force manifest in rape, concubinage, prostitution and (patriarchal) marriage can only occur in a state-centred context.[13] The state's claim to exercise a monopoly of force means that it is not merely one patriarchal institution among many. It holds the *key* to a concept of sovereignty in which men dominate women as an integral part of those hierarchical and divisive processes which marginalize some at the expense of others.[14]

Allen notes the importance of differentiating a whole range of institutions – the police, prisons, the judiciary, social policy agencies, education, labour, industry – that are sometimes seen as part of the state.[15] She points out that these institutions pull in different directions, and in her analysis of abortion policy in Australia she notes the twists and turns of an administration whose policies are a mixture of the progressive and the patriarchal. But what Allen demonstrates, in my view, is not the irrelevance of the state, but the importance of defining it *strictly* as an institution which claims a monopoly of legitimate force. Once we do this, it becomes possible to distinguish (at least analytically) between agencies which merely administer in governmental terms, and those which stand ready to use force if all else fails. Contradictions arise because analytically distinct governmental institutions act in tension with the state.

Policies empower women when they provide resources and reform male-only institutions. Such policies are, strictly speaking, *governmental* (rather than statist) in character since they work against the need for force. Robert Connell argues that a feminist state in which some rule over others would be a contradiction in terms. But this point leads him not to challenge the state itself, but to argue instead for what he calls a feminist state which provides 'an arena for a radical democratization of social interaction'.[16]

The problem here is the one we encountered with Held's analysis of democracy. If we define the state simply in governmental terms, we gloss over its reality as an institution which, in claiming a monopoly of legitimate force, asserts a sovereignty which has a divisive and distinctively patriarchal character.

Jones and the 'sovereignty trap'

For Jones, the 'sovereignty trap' arises when authority is construed in a hierarchical and exclusionary manner. Hobbes, she argues, makes it impossible to understand how individuals relate to one another as members of a common community since he treats social relationships in terms of a command–obedience framework.

In Jones's view, Hobbes defends patriarchy because he assumes that authority can only take the form of sovereignty. Authority is monolithic, and it would be impossible for Hobbes's body politic to be represented by 'a dividing, birthing body'. Hobbesian sovereignty is masculinist, not simply because it ascribes leadership to men (which it does), but because it conceives of authority in this unitary and monolithic way.[17] The question central to Jones's argument is this. Can authority be conceptualized in a feminist rather than a patriarchal manner? To feminize authority, she argues, we must overcome the traditional liberal dichotomy between compassion and authority, feeling and cognition, empathy and judgement. Leadership conceived in a feminist fashion involves communication and dialogue, not dictation and command,[18] and the concept which particularly feminizes authority for Jones is the notion of *compassion*.

Compassion links authority to 'emotive connectedness'. In place of authority as a distant, dispassionate and disciplinary gaze, we are involved with an 'imaginative taking up of the position' of the 'other'. The fact, Jones argues, that another's problems are distinct does not mean that I cannot perceive this suffering '*as if* it were my own and work in solidarity with unique others toward certain goals'. The language of compassion, 'taken into the public realm, can be made into the language, not of violence, but of protective peacemaking'. The Copernican revolution which transforms authority, needs to embrace concepts of freedom and equality, justice and power as well.[19]

However, as far as Jones is concerned, sovereignty can only be formulated in masculinist, hierarchical and monolithic terms.[20] But why? Why can't we reconceptualize the concept so that it expresses a notion of autonomy that is 'compassionate'? Why should sovereignty constitute a *trap* which necessarily involves arrogance, hierarchy and a patriarchal authoritarianism?

Sovereignty and *The Second Sex*

It is clear from Jones's argument that women can only liberate themselves by challenging the (repressive and statist) sovereignty of men. But once we focus on the question as to how an oppressive male sovereignty is to be transformed we are obliged, it seems to me, to engage with the fact that sovereignty, like authority, justice, power and autonomy, can also be reconceptualized.

In this regard Simone de Beauvoir's classic analysis of men and women in *The Second Sex* is revealing. In the main, de Beauvoir sees sovereignty as the attribute of men who dominate women. She identifies it with male privilege. In situations in which women are complicit with patriarchy, become powerful rulers themselves, or exercise some power within a domestic sphere, the term sovereignty denotes domination. Sometimes sovereignty is associated with violence, and often with religion. There is a particularly powerful characterization of sovereignty as a statist quality when de Beauvoir speaks of the solitary and isolated efforts of women to exchange their servitude for a sovereign liberty, while leaving the framework of a patriarchal society intact.[21]

But if the concept of sovereignty normally denotes repression and domination in *The Second Sex*, it does not always do so. At one point, de Beauvoir describes a man who sees himself as superior to his female companion, as 'well pleased to remain the sovereign subject'. At the same time she argues that when a woman seeks to destroy male superiority, she demands 'the reestablishment of her sovereignty'.[22] This implies a domination in reverse but not quite. In terms of Hegel's famous 'dialectic' (to which de Beauvoir alludes) in which masters depend upon slaves, the woman is the slave. She wishes to emerge into what de Beauvoir calls 'the light of transcendence'. Women do not seek to drag men into 'immanence' so that, in this example at least, the sovereignty of (emancipated) women is qualitatively different from the sovereignty of (patriarchal) men. Women assert the sovereignty of slaves who are liberating themselves – not the sovereignty of masters who act at the expense of others.

A qualitatively different notion of sovereignty is even more clearly expressed elsewhere in de Beauvoir's argument. In her analysis of adolescence, she argues that for the young woman, 'there is a contradiction between her status as a real human being and her vocation as a female'. Once an autonomous individual, 'now she must renounce her sovereignty'.[23] Here, it seems, sovereignty does not simply invert domination by substituting one oppression for another. Rather it is about women having control over their own lives. De Beauvoir speaks of the woman within the familial household inhabiting a realm 'where she can control things and in the midst of which she enjoys precarious sovereignty'. The implication here is that in this (admittedly rather unappealing) situation, women enjoy a 'precarious' freedom that is different in kind from the repressive and exploitative sovereignty which patriarchal men exert.

When the term 'sovereign subject' is identified with men, it denotes violence, tyranny and possessiveness. On the other hand, when de Beauvoir analyses the plight of a supposedly emancipated woman within a patriarchal society, the term has a different meaning. In order to realize her femininity, de Beauvoir comments, this woman 'must renounce her claims as sovereign subject'.[24] This, it seems to me, is just one of a number of passages in *The Second Sex* in which sovereignty does not mean a capacity to dominate others.

Feminizing sovereignty

Brace makes explicit what is implicit in de Beauvoir. The sovereignty of the individual can take different and contradictory forms. Brace takes Hobbes as the classic exponent of a masculinist individuality, but argues that feminists can learn from the seventeenth-century radical, Gerrard Winstanley, in forging new conceptions of the self and sovereignty.

While neither Hobbes nor Winstanley discuss the question of self-sovereignty directly, the imagery they use is suggestive. Whereas Hobbes sees individuals as competitive and atomistic, Winstanley insists upon the importance of unity, community and relatedness. The relevance of Winstanley, Brace argues, is that he embraces a discourse which acknowledges common interests, allows for overlapping domains and rejects the idea of mastery and dominion.[25] For Hobbes, the autonomy of the individual is like the autonomy of the state. It involves distrust, fear, subjugation and of course force. Relationships are accidental and artificial, and individuals inhabit state-like territories insulated from others. Winstanley, by contrast, speaks of a 'domain' (rather than a territory) in which sovereign individuals connect to and work with others. What makes Winstanley helpful, Brace argues, is his relational view of sovereignty. In other words, the kind of arguments which Jones uses to reconceptualize authority can be used to reconceptualize or 'reclaim' sovereignty as well.[26]

Brace's analysis meshes in well with the argument advanced by Offen. For Offen seeks to define feminism by drawing upon both the 'relational' feminism of the continental European tradition and the 'individualist' feminism of Anglo-American culture. Her argument is that when one of these traditions is posed against the other, feminism suffers from the deficiencies and one-sidedness of both.

Relational feminism has traditionally stressed the rights of women as a distinctive group defined by its child-bearing and/or nurturing capacities. 'Difference' is linked with a static view of nature, support for the state and a casual attitude towards personal freedom. On the other hand, the individualistic tradition emphasizes the importance of women as persons with equal rights, but, in so doing, it ignores the subjugating realities of most women's lives.[27] Both traditions need to find a place within feminism.

Building on the liberal tradition

Offen identifies feminism with the notion of 'self-sovereignty'. The concept of individual sovereignty is an important idea, but to sustain it we need to disentangle this individualism from the hierarchical, statist and patriarchal dimensions embodied in the liberal tradition.

In caring for others, individuals, it has been argued, should displace their own interests and become engrossed with the reality of those for whom they care. But Brace warns that this argument has an illiberal and abstractly communitarian character, and she draws upon the positions of Winstanley and Drucilla Cornell to argue for a notion of sovereignty which embraces the kind of individuality which allows us to 'imagine and reimagine ourselves on our own terms'.[28] In other words, a feminist view of sovereignty must respect both individuality *and* difference. Power and politics remain essential to social relationships precisely because differences generate tensions, and conflicts continuously need to be resolved. Relationships are not only undermined when one individual imposes their will upon another. They are also undermined when one yields to another in a way which denies a distinct identity. Jennifer Nedelsky argues that the image of skin (rather than walls) better captures the idea of a boundary within a relationship since the point about skin is that it is permeable and sensitive to context. As Brace comments wryly, 'we need to reclaim some kind of sovereignty from the ideal of selflessness, otherwise we are going to find far too many people getting under our skin'.[29]

In reconceptualizing sovereignty in a feminist manner, it is crucial that we build upon and not reject the individualism of the liberal tradition. Sovereign individuals are those who relate to others as distinct, egalitarian and autonomous beings. Cynthia

Daniels has attacked the notion of foetal rights – the idea that the baby in the womb has 'rights' which are independent of the wishes of the woman carrying it. Such a notion, she contends, constitutes an attack on a woman's 'self-sovereignty' – that is, her right to bodily integrity. It is, as she points out, particularly poor women, women of colour and women from non-Western cultures whose bodies are liable to be treated as the property of the state. When pregnant women act in ways which damage the foetus they are carrying, they are engaging in self-abuse, and Daniels argues that resorting to prosecution in situations like these merely undermines the self-sovereignty of women as members of a democratic community.[30]

The assertion of this self-sovereignty threatens patriarchal power. Daniels makes an eloquent case for the kind of polity which affirms the right of individuals to autonomy through social development. What is problematic about her argument, however, is that she characterizes this self-sovereignty as the most fundamental of *liberal* rights, and she talks about the 'demasculinization' of the public world in terms of developing a *state* which supports not the politics of vengeance but a culture of compassion.[31] Liberal rights are part of a statist tradition which naturalizes force. We can only build upon this tradition by moving beyond it. The point about self-sovereignty, as Daniels graphically indicates, is that it is undermined by the use of force as a way of resolving conflicts of interest.

A feminist view of sovereignty can only be coherent, therefore, if it explicitly contests the logic and viability of an institution which claims a monopoly of legitimate force. A sovereignty based upon compassion, egalitarianism, a respect for difference and an understanding of how individuals identify themselves through social relationships, is a sovereignty which has broken with the repressive and hierarchical logic of the state.

8
Postmodernism

Postmodernism is, I want to argue, imbued with a logic that is anti-authoritarian and anti-statist in character. It has an important role to play in developing sovereignty as a post-statist concept. In 'deconstructing' state sovereignty, a new style of critique itself is necessary. It is crucial that we avoid timeless assumptions, static 'foundations' and a notion of freedom and emancipation which is itself abstract and unreal in character.

The subversive 'logic' of postmodernism is often in tension with the particular positions of particular practitioners. If postmodernism is to contribute positively to the formulation of a post-statist concept of sovereignty, it needs to recognize the centrality of modernism and the modernist conception of sovereignty.

Statism and the philosophical critique

The concern which postmodernists have with abstraction and absolutism makes a 'definition' of postmodernism especially problematic. One writer has focused specifically upon *postmodernity* but concedes that 'postmodernism and postmodernity must be viewed in terms of each other'. Another has sought to differentiate between postmodernism and post-structuralism, suggesting that 'postmodernism is to art what poststructuralism is to philosophy and social theory'. However, I propose to follow a broad view of postmodernism which has recently been characterized as a 'convergence' of theories of art, post-structuralism and perspectives on the post-industrial society.[1]

R.B.J. Walker warns of 'totalising strategies' towards defining postmodernism which stress convergences at the expense of differences.[2] This problem can be tackled, in my view, by constructing a 'logic' which enables us to take account of the postmodernist critique, while at the same time noting the divergencies and discrepancies which arise as individual practitioners resist the full implications of this logic. All postmodernists are critical of static and hierarchical modes of thought. What they specifically target are those propositions which express themselves in a 'dualistic' or exclusionary manner.

Rooted in Western thought (and going back to the ancient Greeks) is the idea that our institutions are structured around antinomies or dualisms. A proposition is dualistic when it presents the world in terms of binary opposites in which one half is deemed 'virtuous' and the other vicious. The relationship between 'opposites' is hierarchical and totalistic. 'Logocentric' discourses are those which (to provide the kind of examples often referred to in the literature) pit in exclusionary terms truth against falsity, unity against diversity, subject against object, men against women, and so on. Either we support one or the other: it is impossible, in logocentric theory, to embrace *both*.

The point about logocentric or monological thought is that it is intolerant and authoritarian. Each binary opposite confronts the other as an 'enemy' to be extinguished – in terms of a zero-sum game in which if one wins, the other loses. I see logocentrism as a conceptual *statism* since the notion fits the Weberian definition of the state like a glove. Lyotard has referred to logocentric propositions as 'grand narratives of legitimation', and the state offers just such a privileged discourse of legitimacy. It is a legitimator which does not itself need to be legitimated. Weber's comment that the state is 'the highest and ultimate thing in the world . . . the highest power organization on earth'[3] highlights the way in which the state needs to be subjected to a philosophical critique of abstract thought.

In challenging the notion that truth comes from on high as the timeless dictums of a conceptual deity, postmodernism questions the legitimacy of the state as an institution which claims the 'right' to impose force from above. Postmodernists conceptualize all knowledge as discourse, and see discourses as theories which exercise power. It is the practical character of theorizing that makes all our thinking political, since politics itself arises from an ongoing awareness of difference. This awareness creates an inevitable tension which politics seeks to resolve. It is clear that postmodernism, in rejecting logocentric and hierarchical modes of thought, is not rejecting politics but rather challenging the state.

Ashley's attack on state sovereignty

Richard Ashley focuses his postmodernist critique on domestic and international politics. Realist and neo-realist theory in international relations, he argues, is premised on the assumption that world affairs can only be centred around the activities of sovereign states. This theory turns on a hierarchical opposition between sovereignty on the one hand and anarchy on the other. Ashley draws upon Jacques Derrida to argue that logocentrism expresses itself as 'a sovereign voice' – a higher reality, a regulative ideal. Anarchy, by contrast, is derivative and negative, and necessarily threatens the ideal of sovereignty.[4]

Ashley's critique focuses on the 'heroic practice' as a discourse which presents itself in starkly oppositional terms. In political theory, sovereignty is pitted against anarchy in a way which demands that we take sides. Either we are in favour of the sovereign state, or we support a shapeless, irrational and destructive anarchy. Ashley acknowledges his indebtness to Michel Foucault, but at the same time he uses the notion of sovereignty much more broadly than Foucault does. Whereas Ashley links state sovereignty with modernism, Foucault identifies sovereignty as a medieval institution in which absolute control is exercised over subjects through an open and explicit display of violence. The rise of surveillance in the seventeenth and eighteenth centuries constituted a new mechanism of power involving instruments, techniques and apparatuses which, Foucault argues, are 'absolutely incompatible with the relations of sovereignty'.[5]

For Ashley, sovereignty is not simply identified with a particular king or ruler. It is a logocentric *principle* – a 'presence' which can be an 'individual actor, a group, a class or a political community'. As far as Ashley is concerned, the sovereign voice embraces an abstract and divisive logic that finds its most consistent and comprehensive expression in the state. The sovereign state is characterized by dogmatism, arrogance and a solipsistic belief that it is the ultimate source of meaning and truth. Sovereign statehood is a legitimate power that defines the basis of its own legitimacy and power.[6]

Not surprisingly, this abstract institution is linked to *force*. Modern discourses of politics view the state 'as a unique and central focus and reserve of violence and rational administration of resources'. The state is distinguished by 'its effective claim to the means of violence'. Force and violence have to be used whenever history refuses to bow to 'sovereign man's reason'. The state is 'the sovereign subject of rational collective violence', and domestic society the 'object domain' subordinated to 'the state's sovereign gaze' – a gaze which necessarily resorts to force to instil discipline and order anarchy.[7]

Deconstruction and dialogue – the problem of alternatives

For postmodernists, an oppressive and dogmatic monologue must be challenged by 'dialogue' or deconstruction. A dialogue opens up new possibilities and constitutes a critique from within. When interrogated in postmodernist fashion, a discourse undermines, undoes, subverts and displaces its own certain and central voices[8] so that it becomes clear that the sovereign state, for example, is part of history, is linked to the anarchy it seeks to exclude, and has legitimations which are themselves in need of legitimation.

The problem with realists, as Ashley points out, is that while they define their values in global terms, they continue to privilege the role of states in general. Hence, a figure like Hedley Bull (whose argument we shall deconstruct later) supports the case for an international society governed by morality and law, but at the same time characterizes this society as an anarchy which stands in contrast to the static and timeless existence of sovereign states.

But logocentrism can also manifest itself in the way we conceptualize competitors to the sovereign state. 'Liberal pluralist discourses of international politics', as Ashley calls them, perceive non-state actors as authoritarian sovereign figures which coexist with states. 'Others' who are not recognized or legitimated as actors within these pluralist discourses, are excluded and marginalized. Thus Marxist, Christian, humanist, radical communitarian and ecological critiques of the sovereign state are still logocentric in so far as they conceive the proletariat, the reformer, the enlightened cleric, or the new social movement as abstract rational actors who oppress and exclude others. Even overt critics of the state are prisoners to logocentrism if they identify the end of the state with the 'end of time' and depict the stateless world as one in which history has been finally and totally subordinated to the human will.[9]

The point which Ashley is making is this. State sovereignty cannot be said to have been deconstructed when one (timeless) narrative gives way to another. If abstract realism is logocentric, so too is abstract utopianism. Deconstruction rejects absolutist solutions whether the 'central autonomous and powerful authorial figure' as Ashley calls it, embraces a world state, a hegemon, natural law, God or the functional imperative of humankind. Deconstruction is only possible when the reader refuses (in Ashley's words) to be 'victimised by a blackmail of the heroic practice' which compels us to choose *either* realism as the practical acceptance of things as they are *or* idealism as a speculative repudiation of objective realities.[10]

A dialogical or deconstructionist critique does not import abstract and timeless principles from outside, but works on the state's own assumptions. It is not the 'critic' who links sovereignty to monopoly, and order to the imposition of 'legitimate force': it is the state itself! Once heroic practices are challenged by a dialogical or deconstructionist stance, it becomes clear, in Ashley's words, that the state is in fact 'a complex amalgam of potentially contesting individuals and agencies'.[11] It is a divided institution wrestling with a multiplicity of opponents whose diversity and plurality are ironically implied by the very existence of the state's sovereign voice. It is not a question, then, of 'choosing' between malevolent states or benevolent statelessness. The abstract character of the state is not eliminated by substituting an equally abstract alternative, for, as I have argued above, as long as we have conflicts of interest which resist negotiation and compromise, the force of the state remains inevitable.

The point, rather, is this. The deconstruction of the state opens up what Ashley calls 'new ways of thinking and doing global politics'.[12] New methods of handling conflicts of interest have to be conceptualized. In deconstructing state sovereignty, it is necessary to demonstrate that it is *the state itself* which raises notions of community and common interest – notions which are at the same time in tension with exclusionary and divisive methods of seeking order.

Without the culture and claims of the state, no move towards a post-statist concept of sovereignty would be possible.

Postmodernism and the problem of relativism

I have presented postmodernism as a subversive logic which challenges the logocentric institutions of the sovereign state. But postmodernism is not necessarily the same as the particular positions embraced by particular practitioners. Postmodernists such as Ashley believe that it is possible to demolish the notion of state sovereignty without formulating an alternative conception. He identifies sovereignty with the state, but fails to explore what sovereignty might look like as a post-statist concept.

This failure to detach sovereignty from the state derives from an endorsement of relativism. Ashley contends that in developing his dialogical reading of the anarchy problematique, he is not seeking to 'impose a standard and pass a judgement'. He argues (as we have noted above) that a dialogical reading allows 'a considerably enriched depiction of the political predicament of modern global politics'.[13] Yet, at the same time, he insists that no 'judgement' is being made of that monological reading of the sovereign state which he remorselessly and skilfully demolishes!

His stance is one of radical scepticism, and it is a stance which leads him to deny the practical implications of his own theory. For Ashley, all theoretical positions are equally arbitrary. Both sovereignty and the state are 'undecidable'. He is not, he tells us, raising 'the tired position of whether theoretical assumptions are "true" or "false"'. On the contrary, all knowledgeable practices are 'arbitrary practices of power by which the proliferation of meaning is disciplined and narrative structure is imposed on history'. The champions of the anarchy problematique have long had their practised response to this 'familiar issue', Ashley argues, and he quotes Waltz's comment that 'assumptions are neither true nor false': all we can say is that they are 'essential for the construction of theory'.[14]

But this is a curious position indeed for a postmodernist to adopt. For Ashley endorses here the philosophical scepticism of a figure who is a major force in neo-realist IR theory and (it goes without saying) a militant modernist to boot! The point is that scepticism and relativism are integral to modernist philosophy. They lie at the heart of positivism and empiricism, and can be found in their 'modern' form in the writing of David Hume. Ironically, the scepticism and relativism which Ashley adopts, tie him to the very institution which he appears to challenge – the sovereign state. If postmodernism is just as arbitrary as every other discourse, then it must follow that it too has a dogmatic 'sovereign voice', imposes 'narrative' structures on history, and embodies a statist logic which seeks to extinguish the diversity it presupposes.[15]

When Ashley argues, for example, that deconstruction does not approach a text on the basis of some 'higher logical principle' or from the 'standpoint of some superior reason', he seems to assume (as his language suggests) that logic and reason are themselves logocentric in character. But, as Yeatman has rightly argued, postmodernists 'desacralise reason: they do not reject it'. While they do reject what Yeatman calls a 'heroic form of reason' (a form which underpins Ashley's notion of the heroic practice), postmodernists still work 'comfortably' with reason as a logic which arises from and is sensitive to historical processes. There are, Yeatman concedes, currents within postmodernism which associate it with 'a nihilistic relativism and anomie', but she urges a deconstructive relationship with modernity so that universalism, rationalism and emancipation can be transformed rather than rejected.[16]

We need to move beyond (rather than simply negate) abstract notions of emancipation and rationality. This is why, as Sandra Harding has argued, we should not assume that by giving up the goal of telling 'true' stories about reality, we must also stop telling less false ones. Why argue that unless something is absolutely and timelessly true, it must be absolutely and timelessly false?[17] The relativists invert modernity rather than transcend it. It is rather like displacing God in order to enthrone the Devil. It involves taking sides and surrendering to the blackmail of heroic practice in precisely the way (as Ashley himself shows) that all sovereign statist voices do.

Those who contend that sovereignty is 'undecidable' or cannot be defined, ultimately adopt a statist view of sovereignty. Here Ashley joins postmodernists such as Weber and Bartelson who, as I commented in Chapter 2, adopt what is in effect a top-down, statist view of existence and meaning. Thus Bartelson structures his argument around a choice of abstract opposites in classic statist fashion. Where conventional modernists choose suprahistorical meaning, Bartelson prefers 'contingency'; in place of reason, he champions randomness; instead of order, he opts for anarchy. But these are precisely the polarized 'choices' which a statist approach to sovereignty imposes, and the problem is that *inverting* a dualistic approach does not enable us to transcend it.

Bartelson tells us that he has approached texts as 'a felicitous positivist'.[18] But this means that like Ashley (who endorses the scepticism of Waltz), Bartelson embraces a relativism that is no more than the *alter ego* of modernist beliefs in an abstract progress and static enlightenment.

Deconstruction and the 'privileging' of modernity

In deconstructing an argument, we need to accept that modernity has to be built upon rather than simply rejected.[19] Ashley provides an excellent example of how deconstruction works in practice when he focuses on the question posed by realists such as Waltz: can we conceive of order without an orderer? How can there be international co-operation in the face of anarchy?[20] This is an important question because it points to a logic which takes us beyond the sovereign state.

It is true, as we have seen, that non-state actors, like states themselves, can banish, exclude and marginalize 'outsiders' in order to maintain their own monopolistic identity. However, once we acknowledge that one sovereign state is constrained by others, an unmistakable seed of conceptual subversion has been sown. For whether these outsiders are states or non-state actors, a 'lateral' image of the state (as Ashley calls it) comes into play which is ultimately incompatible with the 'vertical' image of the state as a self-contained agent in full control of its destiny.

When a sovereign state is constrained by others, the question arises: what has happened to those 'absolute boundaries unambiguously demarcating a domestic "inside" and setting it off from an international "outside"'?[21] The presence of plurality in interstate and international relationships casts doubt upon the traditional concept of the sovereign state. However, all this assumes the existence of a modern world in which separate and equally sovereign states have emerged. Pre-modern discourse has no conception of an international society composed of independent sovereign states, and takes it for granted that an interventionist and overarching divinity remains intact.

So why does the idea of an international 'society' implicitly subvert the state sovereignty it purports to defend? On the one hand, Bull (like Wight) does not challenge the idea that international society is composed of sovereign states.[22] On the other hand, Bull not only assumes that the claim to sovereignty by one state is conditional on its recognition by other states, but also specifically focuses on what he calls 'awkward facts' for a state-centric theory of world politics. International law, regional associations, secessionist tendencies, transnational organizations of a technical, scientific, economic and political kind, all challenge the notion that states can exercise the kind of autonomy identified historically with the notion of state sovereignty. Indeed, Bull even concedes that, carried to its logical extreme, the doctrine of human rights 'is subversive of the whole principle that mankind should be organised as a society of sovereign states'.

Bull attempts to reconcile sovereignty with his concept of an international society, but the result is a failure. Sovereignty is conceived as a statist attribute, and states, Bull tells us, are *internally* sovereign when they exercise absolute control over their own territory and inhabitants, and *externally* sovereign when they enjoy 'not supremacy but independence of outside authorities'.[23] But it is not difficult to raise in response to this argument yet another awkward question: if a state lacks supreme power over other states and non-state actors, how can it be said to exercise supreme power over its own citizens?

Bull's own pessimistic conclusion – 'it is better to recognise that we are in darkness than to pretend that we can see the light' – is an exquisite example of logocentric thought. (How can we know one except in relation to the other?) Deconstructing Bull demonstrates the centrality of modernity to postmodernity. He upholds state sovereignty but within an anarchical society ordered by international law and transnational organizations. He espouses a static and ahistorical notion of common interests as the 'empirical equivalent' to natural law theory in what he acknowledges is a dynamic and changing world. He characterizes states as independent, equal and self-determining institutions,[24] but admits that none of these rather desirable attributes can be found in reality.

The point is that Bull can only be so fruitfully deconstructed because he is a *modern* theorist. Bartelson has argued that modern sovereignty 'contains both a prophecy of interstate anarchy and a promise of cosmopolitan redemption'. This comment reinforces my argument. To go beyond modernity, we must first 'privilege' it. 'Interstate anarchy' rests upon the formal equality of states. However, since this equality is not real, we are understandably encouraged to look to 'cosmopolitan redemption' – an order which goes beyond the sovereign state.

This is precisely what Bull does. In what his critics have called a 'tantalizingly brief' passage in the first chapter of his *magnum opus*, he contends that world order – 'order among mankind' – is more fundamental, primordial and morally prior than order among states. The 'ultimate units of the great society of all mankind are not states (or nations, tribes, empires, classes or parties) but individual human beings'.[25] This invocation of a 'morally prior' world order does imply that states cannot be accepted as legitimate actors on their own terms. On the other hand, the notion of individuals as 'ultimate units' points to an abstract moralism which embraces a concrete endorsement of the state. If state sovereignty is to be deconstructed, then the alternative to this state sovereignty cannot itself be logocentric in character.

Bull's notion of justice as a timeless set of communal values in hapless and tragic conflict with the order imposed by states, simply juxtaposes two metanarratives – one 'idealistic', the other rooted in the world of 'realism'. Whereas Bull's doubts about the state express themselves in terms of an abstract concept of individual rights and duties, postmodernism compels us to find a notion of sovereignty that is historical and 'dialogical' in character.

The fact that postmodernists often ground their own arguments in relativism simply indicates how vulnerable they are to the very processes of deconstruction they support. For postmodernism has a logic which is both critical *and* realistic. Deconstruction, as a consistently critical method, rejects the idea that we have to choose between the two, and hence has a crucial role to play in formulating a post-statist concept of sovereignty. If this view of deconstruction does not necessarily commend itself to some of the practitioners of postmodernism, that is because they have been tempted to invert, rather than actually move beyond, the modernist assumptions which they so eloquently challenge and criticize.

Naturalism and Individual Sovereignty

Sovereignty, I have argued, needs to be detached from the state. It is of course possible to conceive of God as sovereign, or males as sovereign or the party as sovereign, but these are hierarchical notions which presuppose the existence of the state. Like other radical ideologies, liberalism conceives of individuals as having a sovereignty which is independent of the state. But although it allows individuals a sovereignty of their own, the liberal notion of the individual suffers from a crucial defect. It is naturalistic, timeless and abstract. As a consequence, the individual is conceived in a way which ultimately requires a state if social order is to be sustained.

Other bodies of thought such as anarchism and Marxism actually challenge the role of the state as the institution which makes order possible. Yet they too embrace abstract positions which conceal repressive hierarchies. The suprahistorical and static concepts which I identify with naturalism, can only undermine the attempt to develop an egalitarian and post-statist notion of sovereignty.

Classical liberalism and the natural individual

What makes the liberal tradition significant in reworking the concept of sovereignty is the argument that all individuals are free, equal and have inalienable rights. States are only legitimate when they have been authorized by consent.[1] Sovereignty is identified not merely in statist but also in individual terms.

In classical liberalism, individuals are depicted as handing the

power of self-government, and thus their own sovereignty, to the
state. The individual, as Hobbes puts it, remains 'Author of all his
Soveraign shall do', and Strauss takes it for granted that this individuality translates into a concept of individual *sovereignty*.[2] But
this does not in itself enable us to detach sovereignty from the state.
Bertrand de Jouvenel notes the link between 'the authoritarian
conclusions of Hobbes' and the 'premises of an absolute liber-
tarianism'; and this point is underlined by Carole Pateman, who
comments that the very abstractness of Hobbes's individualism
meshes logically with his case for an absolutist state.[3] Hobbes's
problem does not derive simply from the authoritarianism of his
state. It derives from the naturalism of his individual, and this is a
problem common to the liberal tradition as a whole.

We accept that Locke's state of nature appears to be a much
more sociable affair than Hobbes's. But for Locke, people have
rights and duties which derive from a 'law of nature' which (as in
Hobbes) is God-given. They are all servants 'of one sovereign
Master' so that sovereignty is hierarchical in conception and divine
in origin. Individuals in Locke's state of nature have the right to
destroy not only 'the inferior ranks of creatures' but also humans.
The power of life and death which they enjoy, is a power of *sovereignty* – conceived in absolutist and statist terms. Slaves can be
legitimately taken as captives in a just war 'by the right of Nature',
and patriarchy is also naturalized.[4] If Locke seeks limited as
opposed to absolute government, his assumptions are essentially
Hobbesian in character. His concern with the protection of property is simply, as Strauss comments, a corollary of Hobbes's fundamental right of self-preservation. Every 'man', Locke argues, has a
'property' in his own 'person', which 'nobody has any right to but
himself'.[5] Property as an extension of self-preservation lies at the
root of individual sovereignty.

The point is that even before the state is introduced into Locke's
argument, we have a concept of individuality which is statist in
character. With the introduction of money and the progressive
removal of all limits to acquisition, the possession of earth becomes
'disproportionate and unequal', and the 'inconveniences' thereby
generated make it inevitable that individuals will require a state.
For Locke, sovereignty involves the absolute control over both
property and the person,[6] and property is an exclusive attribute
which one individual can possess at another's expense.

Rousseau and the concept of an abstract human nature

What makes Rousseau a prisoner of the classical liberal tradition is the naturalism of his argument. All individuals possess, in Rousseau's view, the fundamental desire for self-preservation. Of course Rousseau is sharply critical of 'fraudulent' social contracts which enable the rich 'legitimately' to rob the poor, and he argues famously that in the authentic social contract everyone 'alienates' everything to the community as a whole. Property as a social institution is linked to the existence of justice and the state. But Rousseau can still speak of lives, liberties and properties as 'the constituent elements' of 'men's' being. Despite the radicalism of his position, he remains wedded, in my view, to the notion that freedom is a desire for property which nothing can change. It is part of human nature itself.[7]

All individuals are to unite themselves with others while remaining as free as they were in the state of nature. The sovereignty enshrined in the social contract is essentially statist since, as Rousseau points out, the interests of individuals necessarily clash in a manner which makes a collective force necessary. If circumstances tend to destroy equality, he observes in a graphic dictum, legislation ought to preserve it. The general will seeks to realize this equality through *force*, ordering and disciplining those 'partial' wills which naturally and necessarily threaten it.[8]

Strauss comments, in his analysis of Rousseau, that 'in order to remain as free in society as he was before, man must become completely "collectivized" or "denaturalized"'. But this is misleading. As far as Rousseau is concerned, humans *remain* possessive individualists, even if a legitimate social contract requires that all own property. All have a natural right to what they need, and the institution of property in society makes one aware 'less of what belongs to others than what does *not* belong to oneself'.[9] The 'sentiments of sociability' without which the social contract cannot function, need a religious, as well as a statist, underpinning. One can no more change this possessive human nature than one can change God himself.[10] Among those likely to be on the receiving end of force in a Rousseauian state (the poor, women and aliens) are dissidents tempted to reject the dogmas of a civil religion.

Sovereignty and the new liberalism

Towards the end of the eighteenth century liberals begin to abandon natural rights and social contract theory. The problem, however, is that they do so not to develop a 'conventional' understanding of individuality, but in order to naturalize the state. Moving from natural rights to a conception of utility, or reformulating rights in a Kantian manner, simply moves liberalism away from the emancipatory and subversive thrust of the classical formulations analysed above.

Thus Hume argues that the state itself has always existed. In naturalizing repressive hierarchy, he makes it impossible to conceptualize sovereignty in a post-statist manner. Tribal chieftains, in Hume's 'sceptical' view, employ force to 'reduce the refractory and disobedient' in a manner which is identical in essence to the actions of all leaders. If later liberals dispensed with the idea of natural law, they did so because they saw the unlimited acquisition of wealth as a factual process[11] which no longer requires the 'anarchical fallacies' of natural rights theory to serve as a conceptual underpinning.

John Austin is famous for his notion of the sovereign as a person or persons which the bulk of society is in the habit of obeying. Law, command, civil society and sovereignty are all mutually interdependent, and this celebrated utilitarian definition takes it as read that sovereignty can only be a statist concept.[12] If utilitarians such as Jeremy Bentham and James Mill moved cautiously towards an acceptance of universal suffrage for males, their conceptions of the individual are rooted in a naturalism which makes the idea of a sovereignty outside the state inconceivable.

The position of John Stuart Mill is more interesting. In his celebrated defence of liberty, he asserts that 'over himself, over his own mind and body, the individual is sovereign'. It is true that Mill takes it for granted that individual freedom must be limited by the state,[13] but at the same time he begins to introduce concepts which are crucial to a post-statist concept of sovereignty. On the face of it his concept of individual sovereignty appears divisive and statist, for Mill takes the view that the 'sovereign many' need to be guided by the 'instructed *one* or *few*'. Yet utility, as he conceives it, is grounded in what he calls 'the permanent interests of man as a progressive being', and in a famous passage he likens human nature to 'a tree, which requires to grow and develop itself on all sides, according to the tendency of the inward forces which make it a living thing'.[14]

How does this emphasis on development affect Mill's conception of individual sovereignty? *On Liberty* is contradictory. On the one hand, social intervention appears permissible only to 'prevent harm to others'. On the other hand, Mill's argument is open to an obvious deconstruction. If society is composed of individuals, how can individuals be sovereign if they act in a way which may not harm others, but is nevertheless *self*-destructive? Mill exposes a crucial ambiguity within liberal naturalism. He argues that the sole end for which humans are 'warranted, individually or collectively, in interfering with the liberty of action of any of their number is self-protection'.[15] But if this is so, does it not follow that individuals require protection against all forms of harm, even when the latter are self-inflicted?

The idea that individuals are free to act in a way which concerns only themselves 'presents no difficulty', Mill comments, 'so long as the will of all the persons implicated remains unaltered'. But if we interpret human nature, and thus the exercise of the human will, developmentally (as Mill does), then we need to take a fresh look at those situations in which individuals enter into engagements 'injurious to themselves'. Mill instances the question of slavery. When we allow people to pursue their own interests, we assume that in so doing they are freely providing for their own good. But when people sell themselves into slavery, they abdicate that liberty, and they forgo 'any future use of it beyond that single act'.[16] The principle of freedom cannot require that people should be free not to be free.

This is a remarkable argument with remarkable implications for liberal naturalism and its statist view of individual sovereignty. People exercise their will in ways which are dynamic and continuously changing. A free action is one which is sustained over time. The essence of Mill's argument is this. While individuals must be allowed to be different (even where this difference seems foolish and unwise), they cannot be permitted either to harm others or undertake actions which undermine their own capacity to be free. 'Society' tolerates activities it judges unwise (for example, drinking excessive alcohol) on the grounds, and only on the grounds, that such individuals can 'recover' from their supposed foolishness and continue to exercise their freedom as before.

In other words, no individual has the sovereign right to destroy their own sovereignty. Freedom must be conceptualized as a quality which individuals exercise in relation both to others and to themselves. It is true that Mill is reluctant to follow through the implications of his own position since he argues that we should consent to limitations on our freedom.[17] His very language conveys the problem. Why are we limiting our freedom when we agree not to act self-destructively?

The classical liberals assumed that as the personal and private property of the individual, freedom could be given away in the same abstract manner in which it was exercised. People become servants, Hobbes argues, not because they are born that way but because, as the 'vanquished', they express in words or 'by other sufficient signes of the Will' that they agree to servitude. Rousseau takes this one step further when he argues that although no one can willingly become a slave, 'the murderer consents to die'.[18] Sovereignty exists as alienable property.

In suggesting that we cannot be sovereign not to be sovereign, Mill's argument not only has significant implications for our conception of freedom but also casts doubt on the legitimacy of the state. Anthony Arblaster has noted that while imprisonment is 'the most blatant and basic way in which someone's liberty can be taken away', 'liberals have for the most part accepted prisons and imprisonment as necessary social institutions for the indefinite future'.[19] What Mill makes clear is that in using force against an individual, we not only are destroying freedom at a particular point in time, but may also be making it difficult, even impossible, for people to express their freedom later. Sovereignty is not a static property which we either possess privately or (as criminals) give away. It is something which *develops*, and sovereignty can only develop if conditions exist which enable people to exercise choice and freedom.

It is because Mill is sensitive to context that he also points to other methods of securing order which do not in themselves destroy freedom. Since we do not live in a state of nature but in a society, everything we do, he acknowledges, affects (even if it does not necessarily 'harm') everyone else. We can and should make it plain to people what we think of their actions through positive sentiments such as admiration or negative ones such as distaste, even contempt. A person, Mill notes, may suffer 'very severe penalties at the hands of others' for faults which concern directly that person alone. Mill identifies these penalties as 'natural', since he argues that 'they are, as it were, the spontaneous consequences of the faults themselves[20] – they have not been purposively inflicted on the individual for the sake of punishment.

In Chapter 5, I characterize these natural penalties as an implicit form of coercion, and Mill's point is that they are indispensable for our self-development. They enable people to learn for themselves. I have also argued that coercion may be more explicitly punitive in character. However, although moral coercion (as Mill calls it) can be more problematic than natural penalties, it still falls short of force, and should not, in my view, be regarded as inherently inimical to freedom. Mill regarded himself as a liberal, but his analysis is significant in the way it points beyond the naturalist conception of the individual as a person whose static and abstract acts inevitably necessitate the use of force to 'limit' the exercise of sovereignty.

Naturalism and the anarchist notion of sovereignty

I have dealt elsewhere with the liberal developments after Mill. They move in the direction of an elitism and authoritarianism which continues the process of naturalizing the state.[21] However, naturalism can also undermine arguments which appear to challenge the necessity of the state.

Anarchists view the individual as sovereign, but this vision is unable to contribute positively to a post-statist concept of sovereignty as long as the critique is based upon naturalist assumptions. Anarchists such as William Godwin embrace a notion of individual sovereignty which denies the existence of social relationships, while Max Stirner's rejection of morality makes it difficult to see how sovereign individuals could possibly order their lives in the absence of the state. Even where anarchists stress the importance of solidarity, they adopt quasi-liberal abstractions which work against a post-statist view of sovereignty. Bakunin declares with an anti-Hobbesian fervour that 'man is born into society, just as an ant is born into an ant-hill or a bee into a hive'. At the same time, he takes the view that sociability and egoism are both 'drives' which are equally necessary 'in the natural economy of beings'.[22]

Sovereignty is conceived in terms of a static concept of human

nature. Governmental processes themselves are inherently oppressive, and all anarchists, 'whatever their persuasion', Marshall
argues, believe in a concept of spontaneous order which leads them
to oppose state and government alike. Anarchists also reject the
need for coercion *per se*. However, as a result of the naturalism
which underpins their arguments, violence and authoritarianism
enter through the back door. Many anarchists are, as April Carter
points out, 'peculiarly receptive' to the appeals of violence, despite
the fact that violence is inimical to anarchist notions of freedom and
autonomy. The point is that violence is inherent in a naturalistic
view of individual sovereignty.[23] An abstract absolutism is unavoid-
able whether we conceive of sovereignty as a natural desire to
appropriate property or as a natural instinct to revolt.

Marshall argues that even in a stateless society, the pressure of
public opinion constitutes a 'political and moral coercion' that anarchists consider unacceptable. Social pressures must give way to
freely adopted customs and norms as a new social order makes disputes 'increasingly unlikely'. Godwin considered public opinion as
a force no less irresistible than whips or chains; Orwell, we are told,
found Tolstoy's pacifism potentially oppressive, while Gandhi's
non-violence is considered to exert a moral force over people which
has authoritarian overtones.[24]

The problem is this. Living in society exposes the individual to a
whole range of coercive pressures which compel people to do things
they otherwise would not have done. Sovereign individuals can
either reject or comply with these pressures, and it is not part of my
argument to assert that particular coercive pressures are necessarily
justified. But the point is that, in some shape or form, these pressures are inherent in all social relationships. They cannot be said to
contradict the exercise of sovereignty. The contrast between coercion and force enables us to conceptualize sovereignty in governmental as opposed to statist terms, and a governmental concept of
sovereignty is only possible if we break with the naturalism of the
anarchist tradition.

Marxism and the spectre of naturalism

It is argued that in 'discovering' communism, Marx merely inverts
the liberal tradition. The individual is 'reduced' to society through
a dream of 'perfect unity' which can only be realized (in Lesek

Kolakowski's words) 'as an artificial unity imposed by coercion from above'.[25] The situation is complicated. There is, I want to argue, a tension between Marx's materialism – which stresses the importance of relationships and a dynamic view of will – and conceptions of communism, production, the proletariat and class struggle which retain naturalistic (and thus statist) features.

Marx's materialism seeks to build upon rather than simply reject the liberal tradition. He speaks of the liberal state representing 'real progress' within the existing order, and he criticizes the idea that society constitutes 'a framework exterior to individuals'. In *The German Ideology* he and Engels specifically challenge the contention that under communism, the sovereignty of the whole suffocates the sovereignty of its parts.[26] Individuality is not jettisoned. It is to be reconceptualized, so that when Marx takes the view that people enter into relations 'independent of their will', he is not denying their capacity to act. He is merely insisting that sovereignty derives from the fact that we cannot survive unless we enter into relationships. The point is that if humans *have* to produce 'in order to sustain human life', then the world cannot be ordered according to an ideal or an idea, however rational or 'compelling'.

This is a materialism which rejects the notion that what happens in the world 'below' depends upon orders, ideals, principles or visions expressed from 'on high'. It rightly identifies a top-down theory of sovereignty with 'the idealism of the state'.[27] While we enter into relationships because we wish to do so, Marx's argument is that our consciousness of what we do is always an imperfect and partial reflection of the complexity of the relationships into which we enter. Sovereignty arises as people try to exert greater control over the world around them through understanding and transforming the relationships which are integral to their identity. As a dynamic concept, sovereignty cannot therefore be conceived as the property of an individual or institution which has 'mastered' history according to the dictums of an abstract reason which stands outside time and place.

But if Marx is right to emphasize the importance of individuals entering into relations of production as a basic condition of life, his notion of production itself is narrowly and naturalistically construed. Production is conceived, for example, in a way which excludes the traditional labour of women in the form of either reproductive activity or the domestic activity of the household. The

division of labour is not taken to embrace gender relations, while
the celebrated comparison in *Capital* between the architect and the
bee presents, it is argued, an abstract and 'voluntarist' view of
unalienated labour which cannot account for the production,
nurture and socialization of children.[28]

This feminist critique of Marxism highlights the way in which a
post-liberal and emancipatory logic comes to grief in abstract,
monopolistic and naturalistic assumptions about human activity. It
might seem odd to speak of naturalism as a spectre haunting
Marxism when communism is projected as a society which strips
individuals of their 'embeddedness in nature'. But the point is that
nature itself is characterized as a female adversary against whom
'man' must wrestle, compelling 'her' forces to act in obedience with
'his' will.[29] A patriarchal view of production is linked to a privi-
leging of class as an explanatory principle, and the proletariat is
seen as the exclusive agent of emancipation. The idea of communism as the end of politics makes it difficult to understand how
conflicts of interest arise in all societies, and require governmental
mechanisms to resolve them.

Tension exists, in other words, between what Di Stefano calls
Marx's 'dialogic' view of history, and the idea of communism as a
'unique destination' in which the inexorable laws of history guarantee the working class final victory. Emancipation is not a political
process in which committed individuals seek to establish alternatives to repression and exploitation. As far as Marx is concerned,
emancipation derives from a historically privileged theory enacted
by agents with a prescribed role to play. This is an anti-statist argument whose naturalistic features give it a pronounced statist character. Nor does it help to add to Marxism, as Antonio Gramsci
does, the concept of hegemony, for hegemony is conceived as a
moral and intellectual concept which stands outside government
and coercion. As a result, the ideal of communism becomes even
more abstract and naturalistic in character.[30]

Ultimately, Marxism presents us with the polarizing 'choice'
between communism as an abstract ideal, and a real world constituted by sovereign states. This choice is resolved in practice in an
authoritarian way. Particular states are given a privileged role to
play in the march to communism, while the transformation of
society is conceived as a revolutionary upheaval which requires
authoritarian organizations to sustain it. It goes without saying that

the more authoritarian the organization, the less likely it is to dissolve itself into the sovereignty of self-governing agents operating at global, regional, provincial and local levels.[31]

If sovereignty is to be conceptualized as a post-statist notion, we need to break from naturalism whether it takes a liberal, anarchist or Marxist form. Just how such an argument might be constructed is explored in my final chapter.

Expounding a Relational View

A relational argument is crucial if a post-statist concept of sovereignty is to be sustained. This means in the first instance *relating* sovereignty to the state and the modernist tradition in which state sovereignty is explicitly articulated. Modernism, I want to suggest, is a necessary, although not a sufficient, condition for a conception of sovereignty which goes beyond the state.

But if states are not sovereign, where then does sovereignty reside? Sovereignty, I want to argue, needs to be identified with individuals rather than states, but this position is only defensible if sovereign individuals are analysed in non-naturalistic terms. Individuality does not exist apart from, but is only manifest through, organizations which are constructed domestically, locally, regionally, nationally and globally – at every conceivable social level. Sovereignty is an absolute concept, but as such it can only express itself in an infinity of relationships across time and space, and these relationships also embrace that wider world of nature of which individuals are an 'organic' part.

Since a relational view of sovereignty is 'integrationist' and inclusive, it must acknowledge that states themselves have a central role to play in making a post-statist concept of sovereignty possible.

The merits of modernity

There is no doubt that the sovereign state is a curious institution, and this makes it tempting to regard it as an irrelevance to the modern world. Bartelson argues that if we want to take the 'relational character' of sovereignty seriously, then 'we must abandon the quest for timeless foundations and essences in political philosophy'.[1] But how can sovereignty be said to have a 'relational character' unless we can identify it? Without the notion of sovereignty as an autonomous, indivisible and individuated entity, how can we begin to construct a post-statist conception?

If sovereignty is to be viewed relationally, it must be 'related' to the real world. This relational argument goes beyond what is conventionally called the 'realist' position, but in the first instance it has to *start* with the acknowledgement that sovereign states cast a long shadow over people's lives. The development of the sovereign state in its modern form from the seventeenth century is indispensable to the relational argument. You cannot look beyond something which does not exist!

Moreover, the presence of countries such as Iraq, Kuwait and Saudi Arabia, for example, warns us against the assumption that the contemporary world is composed exclusively of modern (that is, liberal or liberal-democratic) states. Nor should we assume that individuals who are critical of liberal orthodoxy, are necessarily motivated by emancipatory aspirations. The point is that the existence of liberal states and liberal attitudes towards the state, is crucial to developing a relational view of sovereignty.

The notion that all states are sovereign implies an equality in the eyes of international law which is central to the case for a post-statist world. Bull has noted that the countries of the so-called Third World invariably see state sovereignty as a bulwark against attempts to rob them of their economic resources and manipulate them through policies of 'neo-colonialism'.[2] It is scarcely surprising that when old empires break up and national liberation movements are successful, these movements transform themselves into sovereign states. Sovereign statehood is premised on egalitarian norms, and linked to respect and self-esteem. Naeem Inayatullah and David Blaney are right to note that the states of the Third World identify formal sovereignty with independence, and these states are among the strongest supporters of sovereignty. Sovereignty, they contend, is 'neither irrelevant nor a malevolent force': it is a goal which is 'unrealized'.[3] But in order to realize a principle, it must first be established.

Sovereignty implies self-determination. Modernism identifies self-determination with the sovereign state. We should not idealize modernity, but neither should we reject it. It is impossible, in my view, to deny nations a right to statist forms of self-determination as long as sovereign statehood remains an organizing principle of international relations. Gidon Gottlieb argues that groups such as the Kurds or Palestinians should accept an internationally recognized territorial status which falls short of statehood, since if the nations of the world all became states, this would aggravate the kind of violence which has erupted since the end of the cold war.

But the problem is this. Why should Kurds and Palestinians, for example, be denied the sovereign statehood which is enjoyed by Iraqis, Iranians, Turks and Israelis? If we allow modernity for some while imposing (what is in effect) pre-modernity for others, this can only ride roughshod over the formal egalitarianism established by the modernist conception of the sovereign state. We need, in other words, to build upon modernism, not reject it. Gottlieb argues that 'the assertion of a national identity is a political and cultural phenomenon'. At the same time, he argues that this national identity should not be confused with state citizenship. But people can only be persuaded to accept political forms of self-determination that are not themselves statist in character in a world in which the principle of statehood itself is openly and explicitly challenged. Gottlieb argues that 'in the abstract a good case can be made for liberal nationalism and for the principle that every nation should have a state of its own',[4] but this is precisely the point. A good case for liberal nationalism and popular statehood *cannot* be made. Once we uncritically endorse the legitimacy of the state for some, it is invidious and untenable to deny statehood to others.

Samuel Barkin and Bruce Cronin suggest that the interpretation placed upon sovereignty depends upon the way in which 'states relate to each other'. They are concerned in particular with the historical tension between what they call 'state sovereignty' which stresses a definite link between sovereign authority and defined territory, and 'national sovereignty' which emphasizes the link with a defined population. While they are right to stress the variable (and contextual) character of sovereignty, their relational argument does not go far enough. The contrast they make between national and state sovereignty is misleading since they also take it for granted that national sovereignty is statist in the sense that it involves *states* tied to nationally defined populations.[5] They raise the question as to whether existing state boundaries should be altered to take account of national groupings which cut across them (for example, the Kurds in Iraq). But not only are national identities themselves more problematic and contestable than Barkin and Cronin assume; the problem which they raise, but cannot resolve, lies basically with the modernist endorsement of the state.

A relational view must build upon modernity by looking beyond it. The modernist view of state sovereignty naturalizes the individual, the nation, the people and force itself. Barkin and Cronin concede that tying nations to states is likely to intensify inter-state violence (as dominant states resist the redrawing of boundaries) while linking sovereignty to existing juridical entities would aggravate violence within states.[6] But the question they ignore is precisely the one they should be addressing – what can be done to tackle this violence itself? This problem cannot be engaged as long as we continue to take the legitimacy of statehood for granted.

No one can deny that deep discrepancies in real power exist between sovereign states.[7] But if the egalitarianism which states enjoy is formal and abstract, it is not irrelevant. The people of South Africa had first to 'constitute' themselves as a modern nation state before they could set about tackling the grim social and personal inequalities which poison their society. Rosenberg is therefore wrong to deny that the abstract equality of modern states has any implication for concrete 'material' practice. On the contrary, it is the division between egalitarian form and unequal reality that provides every emancipatory movement with its case for change. Rosenberg denies that the egalitarianism of universal suffrage poses a challenge to the class hierarchies of capitalism.[8] But this is untrue. The emancipatory movements of the contemporary world, whether we think of new liberals, trade unionists, socialists, communists, feminists, ecologists, or anarchists, all challenge class hierarchies precisely because these movements take the existence of a formal statist egalitarianism for granted.

A relational view of sovereignty must develop a critique on two fronts. On the one hand, it needs to contrast modernist conceptions of individuality and equality with the explicit hierarchies and formal inequalities of pre-modernity. On the other hand, it has to pin-point the *post-statist* sovereignty which is struggling to emerge from the contradictory logic of the liberal state. It is not a question of rejecting the importance of modern states and the liberal assumptions upon which they rest. It is a question of going beyond them.

The individual as a collectivity of relationships

The modernist notion of sovereignty as absolute, illimitable and indivisible is crucial if the concept is to be coherently developed. Our understanding of sovereignty is not advanced by an argument that sovereignty must be limited, divided up or shared, for the point is that modernity can only be built upon if we break with a polarized argument which implies that the only alternative to modernity is a retreat to pre-modernity. James is therefore right to insist in his defence of modernity that either we are sovereign or we are not.[9]

The problem with modernism is not its absolute concept of sovereignty *per se*. The problem is rather that this absolutism is identified with naturalized conceptions of the individual, the nation and the state. Sovereignty is vested in a particular institution or grouping. While the relational argument requires a concept of sovereignty which is absolute, we need to recognize that precisely because such a concept is absolute, it is also *infinite* in character.

Individuals acquire their freedom and autonomy through their relations with others. Since relationships are ongoing and in a process of continual change, identities are fluid and malleable. It is this relational quality which gives individuality its 'conventional' and 'artificial' character. The contention that persons 'are natural entities' whereas states are not, is quite unhistorical. Larry Siedentop has argued that the individual should be conceived as a 'social construct' – a 'cultural achievement' – and what he calls the naive notion of 'natural individuals' is tied to the atomism and physicalism of the seventeenth and eighteenth centuries.[10] Individual identities only emerge when, as a result of market relationships, people see each another as interchangeable and equal. Identity is constructed through relationships which manifestly differ from the explicitly hierarchical encounters characterizing pre-liberal societies.

The liberation of the individual from explicit hierarchy is, I have argued, a precondition for a post-statist concept of sovereignty. However, it is not enough. For the naturalism of a possessive market society transfers the divinity associated traditionally with particular rulers to the individual. We are still left with the problem of an absolute concept embodied paradoxically in historically relative form. Static and atomistic conceptions of the individual exclude those who are therefore forced by the state to be 'free'.

A relational view of sovereignty sees individuals as continuously reappraising the view they take of others, and continuously reappraising the view they take of themselves. As an absolute concept, sovereignty can only manifest itself developmentally, dynamically, and through identities which are in a process of change. Once force is used, this fluid and interpenetrating quality is disrupted, and a stark hierarchy between subject and object emerges. Sovereign individuals can no more repress others than they can repress themselves,[11] for the use of force destroys dialogue and interchange, whether this is conceived as occurring between individuals, or within the individual (whose self-relationships are also infinite).

Relationships involve both entitlements which empower, and norms which restrict. Mill's notion of 'natural penalties' (which we have already commented upon) is relational because it focuses upon the way in which people are affected by their relationships with others (and indeed themselves) and are therefore continuously changing (or resisting change) as a consequence.

Relationships enable people to change places – to put themselves in each other's position. It is wrong to assume that relationships take only one form. Relationships are multi-layered, and in a world in which communication increasingly occurs on a global scale, individuals concentrate within themselves a dense network of relationships which is expanding all the time. The individual who joins Amnesty International, for example, sees the individual tortured by military rulers in Argentina or Pinochet's Chile as 'part' of themselves, as someone who has entered their universe of relationships. The person who is moved by the plight of Anne Frank under the Nazis, reaches out through time and space to identify an injustice that necessarily challenges their own sense of freedom and autonomy. Sovereignty involves a continuous and ongoing development in which asserting greater control over one's own life is only possible through a concern with the freedom and autonomy of others.

Just as sovereignty embraces a relationship with other individuals who suffer, so it involves a relationship with those who act in concert to remedy this suffering through institutions or groups which exist locally, provincially, regionally, nationally and/or globally. The relational argument cannot arrest or fix sovereignty by chaining it to this rather than that institution. As an absolute concept, sovereignty can only manifest itself through an *infinite* quest for self-government. Since this quest is conceived in relational terms, it cannot be restricted to a particular person, institution, country, nation, time or place.

Sovereignty and ecological security

Naturalism, as I have defined it, assumes a notion of nature which is fixed and unchanging. A non-naturalist view of sovereignty is one therefore which asserts a link between sovereignty and nature in dynamic and historical terms. In Chapter 7 I noted the views of those who think of boundaries as a permeable skin rather than an impenetrable wall. Just such an analogy is used by Patricia Mische in her argument for ecological security.

It is crucial, she contends, to conceptualize sovereignty as development, and not simply as instant gratification. A sense of history sensitizes us to our relationships not only with the past but also with the future. We must concern ourselves with the well-being of those who come after us. Moreover, this respect for relationships is not simply confined to humans, since the capacity of individuals to govern their own lives is inextricably linked to an ongoing relationship between ourselves and nature. If security is defined as freedom from danger – as safety – then we need to recognize the terrible danger which confronts us from what Mische calls 'new threats to human life emanating from human assaults on the Earth'.[12]

This is more than a question of acknowledging the threat which war (and especially nuclear war) poses to the environment. Human assaults on nature are 'of a new kind and scale' as they threaten to deplete the ozone layer; bring uncontrollable changes in climate through a global greenhouse effect; and pollute water, air and soils, thus contributing to cancers and genetic damage. Vicious circles proliferate. The loss of topsoil and increasing desertification, to take just two examples, bring hunger and starvation for millions, making it more difficult for poorer and exploited parts of the world to contribute to programmes aiming to restore the environment. The destruction of rain forests depletes the earth's oxygen supply and further augments the build-up of carbon dioxide which in turn creates the greenhouse effect.[13]

The question of ecological security compels us to rethink the nature of sovereignty. Sovereignty, Mische argues, should be understood not in terms of states or territories but 'as a dynamic, interactive process involving a system of relationship and flow of energy and information between different spheres of sovereignty'. Unless we define the notion of sovereignty so that it embraces our relationships with the earth as a living system, then the survival of humans themselves is placed in doubt. We are just beginning to understand what Mische calls the deeper laws upon which the future of humans depends, and to which 'all human sovereignties owe allegiance'.[14] If sovereignty is, as I have argued, an absolute concept, it can only manifest itself in infinite terms.

Sovereignty involves the dynamic interrelationship between at least four different spheres. Mische distinguishes between the *biosphere* embracing the air, soil, rock, minerals and waters of the earth; the *technosphere*, which involves communication, industry, agriculture, technology, and so on; a *sociosphere*, in which people relate to one another (and the other two systems) through political and cultural institutions; while some have talked of the *noosphere*, a fourth realm constituted by mind and spirit.[15] Does this mean, then, that humans are not sovereign, but that sovereignty lies with nature and the biosphere?

Mische does speak of 'the sovereignty of the Earth' and she argues that the fundamental flaw of modern philosophies of sovereignty is that they locate sovereignty with humans – kings, parliaments or peoples – thereby limiting sovereignty to 'territorial confines'. But the problem with (what she calls) a 'homocentric' view of sovereignty is this. It works against the well-being and survival of humans themselves. Humans are part of a wider world of nature, so that, as Mische puts it, ecological security is 'security for all humanity'.[16] People cannot become sovereign unless they become conscious of, and act to protect, the wider systems without which they cannot survive. Unless we relate to ourselves and other humans in ways which do not damage and destroy this environment, then we will not be able to relate to anyone or anything at all.

Robert Garner has argued that the concept of sovereignty should be extended to 'at least some nonhuman animals', and that the notion that sovereign individuals have to be human is 'anthropocentric'. But it seems to me that it is unnecessary to argue that some animals – for example, mammals which are at least one year old[17] – are themselves relational and capable of sovereignty. All that needs to be shown is that human relationships are not confined to humans alone: they embrace a wider world of nature itself.

Precisely because the relational argument is sensitive to context, it is concerned with the impact upon sovereignty of both time and space. The mortal threat which the 'human assault' on the environment poses, is a particular product of (in Mische's words) our own 'critical juncture in history'.[18] To take just one of a myriad of pressing examples, it is only as we see how damaging the private car is to the fabric of our social and natural world that we are compelled to think of alternatives. Humans are linked to nature, but in ways which are fluid, continuously changing and thus relational in character.

Moving beyond state sovereignty

Robert Jackson has defined 'Third World' countries as quasi-states on the grounds that they lack the empirical conditions for a 'substantial and credible statehood'. They possess, he argues, negative rather than positive sovereignty. In contrast, he finds that 'substantial political systems' (by which he means liberal states) are prosperous and cultivated, have domestic authority and are credible internationally.[19]

The relational argument, however, identifies the realities of state sovereignty in order to transform them. Respecting realities requires not idealization but *deconstruction*. Mark Hoffman contends that utopias are necessary for the world in which we live 'since they point to a gap between human potential and the reality of human practices', and he quotes Machiavelli's dictum 'where there is no vision, the people will perish'.[20] But this argument makes it sound as though we have a *choice* between stressing potential and acknowledging realities. A relational view seeks to expound a 'utopian realism' which looks for the potential *in* the reality. It is only through engaging with the realities of the state itself that we can conceptualize sovereignty in post-statist terms.

The modern liberal state (rightly) emphasizes the capacity of individuals to govern their own lives, and therefore acknowledges (even if it is powerless to resolve) the tension between force and freedom. The prestige and the leadership of modern states depends upon sustaining and developing these liberal values. Hence states themselves have an interest in strengthening the sense of community, the cohesiveness of relationships, which makes a post-statist concept of sovereignty possible. Paradoxically, as Richard Falk has commented, the state must give way to a variety of what he calls 'alternative ordering frameworks' if it is to remain effective: 'the more willingly and forcefully it does so, the more its legitimate sphere of authority can be sustained'.[21]

Empowering individuals gives states legitimacy; it also makes states redundant. States can only preserve their independence and their influence if they act in ways which ultimately strengthen the capacity of individuals to assert a sovereign control over their own lives. This is why recognizing the reality of state sovereignty is the only way to move beyond it. As Inayatullah and Blaney argue, the critique must come from within. States, they contend, are integral parts of a global structure of production. Because of a functionally and hierarchically differentiated global division of labour, states are unable to 'achieve sovereignty substantively'. Wealthy members of the so-called First World benefit from technological and scientific advantage and from the cheap raw materials and unskilled labour which poor countries provide. If sovereignty is to be realized in such a world, the concept needs to be rethought in relational terms[22] since, Inayatullah and Blaney argue, we are obliged to accept that all states have a right to a wealth which is, after all, collectively and globally produced.

It is not a question of abandoning sovereignty. It is a question of realizing it, and sovereignty cannot be realized in global terms unless we rework the concept itself. Realizing sovereignty 'appears at once, as the fulfilment of an aspiration and the transcendence of the system constricting that aspiration'. States have a vital role to play in developing a 'social responsibility and action',[23] Inayatullah and Blaney argue, which moves us beyond the whole concept of sovereignty as the exclusive, hierarchical and divisive attribute of the state.

Ironically, the Hobbesian argument itself helps here. Hobbes is surely right to insist that without order, life is nasty, brutish and short. However, his naturalism and what Macpherson calls his 'market model of society'[24] make it impossible to conceive of order in relational terms since Hobbes's individuals are incapable of acting as members of a community. As a consequence, the force of the state is necessary, and legitimacy and order become problematic. Yet the *logic* of the Hobbesian argument points to the fact that we have a common interest in avoiding the war of all against all. As states work to strengthen these common interests – in working for peace, improving the environment, tackling global inequalities of wealth, and so on – so they create an orderly world which develops the sovereignty of all. Common interests make it possible to settle differences without resorting to force.

Of course, such interests do not exclude the existence of conflict. On the contrary, it is precisely because each individual is unique and different, that tensions arise, power is exercised and conflicts need to be resolved. The point is that force only comes into play where common interests have yet to be cohesively forged. Force has a self-dissolving role. It should be used only to secure space for policies which cement community so that non-violent and thus non-statist methods of resolving conflicts become effective. What has made us increasingly aware of the futility of force as an end in itself are changes in our own historical situation. Developments in technology make it feasible for disaffected minorities and groups to utilize force of a deadly and highly destructive kind. Continuing reliance upon state sovereignty as the mechanism for securing order can only plunge us still further into a Hobbesian nightmare of chaos and self-destruction.

It is interesting that Mische invokes the principle of 'subsidiarity' in her case for 'global governance'[25] – a principle which stresses that whatever can be handled locally should be. The point is a crucial one. A relational view of sovereignty requires both a centralization and a decentralization of power since the implementation of policies which create sovereignty cannot assume that problems have a fixed or simple location. A government, Mill writes, 'cannot have too much of the kind of activity which does not impede, but aids and stimulates, individual exertion and development'. Paul Hirst is right to argue that the 'core of genuine sovereignty' involves distributing power so that it can be effectively exercised at each of the levels of 'governance' (national, subnational and supranational) 'with the minimum of friction between them'.[26]

If states have a crucial role to play in transcending statism, this role can only be understood when we disentangle the atomistic notion of the state from the relational concept of government. For states move beyond statism as they act in a 'governmental' manner by promoting policies which make the use of force increasingly redundant. There is no reason to fear that increasing integration into the EU will undermine national sovereignty provided this integration strengthens common interests, enables us to exert increasing power over own lives and thus assists in the transition from state to government.

Hinsley's classic definition of sovereignty as the absolute and final authority of the political community[27] must be reformulated in a relational manner. Sovereignty is multi-layered and plural. It is at once individual and collective; personal and social; national, local and global. It cannot be fixed or grounded in a specific institution. Hence, it must be detached from the state. As a relational concept, the one thing sovereignty cannot have is an exclusive and exclusionary character.

Notes

Chapter 1

1 Kenneth Waltz, cited by Justin Rosenberg, *The Empire of Civil Society* (London: Verso, 1994), p. 127.
2 John Hoffman, *Beyond the State* (Cambridge: Polity, 1995).
3 Laura Brace and John Hoffman (eds), *Reclaiming Sovereignty* (London: Pinter, 1997). Laura Brace thought up the title.
4 Alan James, *Sovereign Statehood* (London: Allen & Unwin, 1986).
5 David Held, *Democracy and the Global Order* (Cambridge: Polity, 1995).
6 Kathleen Jones, *Compassionate Authority* (New York and London: Routledge, 1993).
7 John Stuart Mill, *On Liberty* (Harmondsworth: Penguin, 1974).

Chapter 2

1 Alan James, *Sovereign Statehood* (London: Allen & Unwin, 1986), p. 3.
2 E.H. Carr, *The Twenty Years Crisis 1919–1939* (Basingstoke: Macmillan, 1978), pp. 230–1.
3 Jens Bartelson, *A Genealogy of Sovereignty* (Cambridge: Cambridge University Press, 1995), p. 13; Stanley Benn, 'The Uses of Sovereignty', *Political Studies*, 3:2, 1955, p. 122. See Samuel Barkin and Bruce Cronin, 'The State and the Nation: Changing Norms and the Rules of Sovereignty in International Relations', *International Organization*, 48:1, 1994. Also Michael Newman, *Democracy, Sovereignty and the European Union* (London: Hurst, 1996), pp. 5–8. Here he distinguishes between *state* sovereignty, *legal* sovereignty, *popular* sovereignty, *popular state* sovereignty, *shared* sovereignty and *divided* sovereignty.

4 Benn, 'The Uses of Sovereignty', p. 122.

5 Aron is cited by James, *Sovereign Statehood*, p. 10, and Haas by Cynthia Weber, *Simulating Sovereignty* (Cambridge: Cambridge University Press, 1995), p. 1.

6 Newman, *Democracy, Sovereignty and the European Union*, p. 15. See also Christopher Lord, 'Sovereign or Confused? The "Great Debate" about British Entry to the European Community Twenty Years On', *Journal of Common Market Studies*, 30:4, 1992, p. 420; Philip Lynch, 'Sovereignty and the European Union: Eroded, Enhanced, Fragmented' in Laura Brace and John Hoffman (eds), *Reclaiming Sovereignty* (London: Cassell, 1997), pp. 43–4.

7 W.B. Gallie, 'Essentially Contested Concepts', *Proceedings of the Aristotelian Society*, 56, 1955–6, pp. 184, 188, 193.

8 Newman, *Democracy, Sovereignty and the European Union*, p. 1.

9 James, *Sovereign Statehood*, pp. 1, 250; Paul Taylor, 'British Sovereignty and the European Community: What is at Risk?', *Millennium*, 20:1, 1991, pp. 79–80; Newman, *Democracy, Sovereignty and the European Union*, p. 13.

10 James, *Sovereign Statehood*, p. 3.

11 Ibid.; F.H. Hinsley, *Sovereignty*, 2nd edn (Cambridge: Cambridge University Press, 1986), p. 2. Michael Fowler and Julie Bunck subtitle their recent book 'The Evolution and Application of the Concept of Sovereignty' while contending that 'sovereignty arguments stress the just and legal sanctity of the state': Michael Fowler and Julie Bunck, *Law, Power and the Sovereign State* (Philadelphia: Pennsylvania University Press, 1996), pp. 157, 163.

12 Bartelson, *A Genealogy of Sovereignty*, pp. 1–2; Weber, *Simulating Sovereignty*, pp. 1–3.

13 David Easton, *The Political System* (New York: Alfred Knopf, 1953), p. 108.

14 John Hoffman, *Beyond the State* (Cambridge: Polity, 1995), pp. 20, 23. For yet another variant of the abandonment thesis, see Charles Beitz, 'Sovereignty and Morality in International Affairs' in David Held (ed.), *Political Theory Today* (Cambridge: Polity, 1991), p. 254.

15 I have explored the problems with Easton's analysis in more detail in John Hoffman, *State, Power and Democracy* (Brighton: Wheatsheaf, 1988), pp. 25–8; and in Hoffman, *Beyond the State*, pp. 26–8.

16 David Easton, *The Analysis of Political Structure* (London and New York: Routledge, 1990), p. 3.

17 Robert Dahl, *Modern Political Analysis*, 4th edn (Englewood Cliffs, NJ: Prentice Hall, 1984), p. 16.

18 Hoffman, *Beyond the State*, pp. 30–1.

19 Rosemary Pringle and Sophie Watson, '"Women's Interests" and the

Post-structural State' in Michèle Barrett and Anne Phillips (eds), *Destabilizing Theory* (Cambridge: Polity, 1992), p. 63.

20 Bartelson, *A Genealogy of Sovereignty*, p. 1. If we were to abandon all contested terms in political science, it has been drily observed, 'the field would be severely impoverished': Marc Williams, 'Rethinking Sovereignty' in Eleonore Kofman and Gillian Youngs (eds), *Globalization* (London: Pinter, 1996), pp. 112–13.

21 Bartelson, *A Genealogy of Sovereignty*, p. 12; Weber, *Simulating Sovereignty*, p. 3. I have also looked at their arguments in John Hoffman, 'Can We Define Sovereignty?', *Politics*, 17:1, 1997.

22 Bartelson, *A Genealogy of Sovereignty*, pp. 28, 48, 50.

23 Weber, *Simulating Sovereignty*, p. 10.

24 Bartelson, *A Genealogy of Sovereignty*, pp. 1, 6, 49.

25 Ibid., pp. 2, 51.

26 Weber, *Simulating Sovereignty*, p. 5.

27 Bartelson, *A Genealogy of Sovereignty*, pp. 14, 15.

28 Gallie, 'Essentially Contested Concepts', pp. 188–93; John Gray, 'Political Power, Social Theory and Essential Contestability' in David Miller and Larry Siedentop (eds), *The Nature of Political Theory* (Oxford: Clarendon, 1983), p. 96. See also Hoffman, *State, Power and Democracy*, p. 9; and Andrew Mason, *Explaining Political Disagreement* (Cambridge: Cambridge University Press, 1993).

29 Thomas J. Biersteker and Cynthia Weber, 'The Social Construction of State Sovereignty' in Thomas J. Biersteker and Cynthia Weber (eds), *State Sovereignty as a Social Construct* (Cambridge: Cambridge University Press, 1996), pp. 2, 11.

30 Hoffman, *Beyond the State*, pp. 65–6.

Chapter 3

1 Barry Buzan, 'The Timeless Wisdom of Realism?' in Steve Smith, Ken Booth and Marysia Zalewski (eds), *International Theory: Positivism and Beyond* (Cambridge: Cambridge University Press, 1996), p. 48. Given the massive literature on realism, Buzan's own bibliography (pp. 63–5) is worth consulting.

2 R.B.J. Walker, 'Sovereignty, Identity, Community: Reflections on the Horizons of Contemporary Political Practice' in R.B.J. Walker and Saul H. Mendlovitz (eds), *Contending Sovereignties* (Boulder, CO and London: Lynne Rienner, 1990), p. 159; Cynthia Weber, *Simulating Sovereignty* (Cambridge: Cambridge University Press, 1995), p. 2; Jens Bartleson, *A Genealogy of Sovereignty* (Cambridge, Cambridge University Press, 1995), pp. 13–14. 'However paradoxical the concept of state sovereignty may seem, it has stood "essentially uncontested" for two centuries or more': Nicholas Onuf, 'Intervention for the Common

Good' in Gene Lyons and Michael Mastanduno (eds), *Beyond West-phalia?* (Baltimore, MD and London: Johns Hopkins University Press, 1995), p. 48.

3 David Easton, 'The Political System Besieged by the State', *Political Theory*, 9:3, 1981, p. 304. This chapter in particular draws upon the arguments in John Hoffman, 'Is It Time to Detach Sovereignty from the State?' in Laura Brace and John Hoffman (eds), *Reclaiming Sovereignty* (London: Cassell, 1997) pp. 9–25.

4 Martin Hollis and Steve Smith, *Explaining and Understanding International Relations* (Oxford: Clarendon Press, 1990), p. 31; Morton Kaplan, *System and Process in International Politics* (New York: John Wiley and Sons, 1957); Hedley Bull, 'International Theory: The Case for a Classical Approach', *World Politics*, 18:3, 1966, pp. 361–77.

5 J.P. Nettl, 'The State as a Conceptual Variable', *World Politics*, 20:4, 1967–8, p. 564.

6 Alan James, *Sovereign Statehood* (London: Allen & Unwin, 1986), pp. 7–8.

7 Martin Wight, 'Why Is There No International Theory?' in Martin Wight and Herbert Butterfield (eds), *Diplomatic Investigations* (London: Allen & Unwin, 1966), pp. 18, 22.

8 Martin Wight, *International Theory* (London and Leicester: Leicester University Press, 1991), p. 7; R.B.J. Walker, *Inside/Outside* (Cambridge: Cambridge University Press, 1993), p. ix.

9 James, *Sovereign Statehood*, pp. 31, 252–4; Robert Jackson and Alan James, 'The Character of Independent Statehood' in Robert Jackson and Alan James (eds), *States in a Changing World* (Oxford: Clarendon Press, 1995), p. 8. See also Bruce Miller, *The World of States* (London: Croom Helm, 1981).

10 James, *Sovereign Statehood*, pp. 6, 8.

11 Wight, 'Why Is There No International Theory?', p. 20. Hans Morgenthau is cited by Justin Rosenberg, *The Empire of Civil Society* (London: Verso, 1994), pp. 16–17. See also M.J. Smith, *Realist Thought from Weber to Kissinger* (London: Louisiana State University Press, 1986), p. 219; Laura Neack and Roger Knudson, 'Re-imagining the Sovereign State: Beginning an Interdisciplinary Dialogue', *Alternatives*, 21, 1996, p. 136; Stephen Krasner, 'Sovereignty and Intervention' in Lyons and Mastanduno, *Beyond Westphalia?*, p. 232.

12 Smith, *Realist Thought from Weber to Kissinger*, p. 221; Rosenberg, *Empire of Civil Society*, p. 24. For my purposes, the distinction which Richard Ashley makes between realism and *neo-realism* is not important. See Richard Ashley, 'The Poverty of Neorealism' in Robert Keohane (ed.), *Neo-realism and Its Critics* (New York: Columbia University Press, 1986), p. 260.

13 Rosenberg, *Empire of Civil Society*, pp. 28, 31.

14 David Long, review of *Sovereign Statehood, Journal of International Studies*, 16:2, 1987, p. 386. Two writers who see state sovereignty as an irrelevance, still find James's analysis 'the most useful for contemporary times': Yale Ferguson and Robert Mansbach, *The State, Conceptual Chaos and the Future of International Relations Theory* (Boulder, CO and London: Lynne Rienner, 1989), p. 43.

15 James, *Sovereign Statehood*, p. 19.

16 Ibid., pp. 49, 53.

17 Ibid., p. 143.

18 Ibid., p. 80.

19 Ibid., p. 40. See also Alan James, 'Sovereignty in Eastern Europe', *Millennium*, 20:1, 1991, pp. 82–3.

20 James, *Sovereign Statehood*, pp. 41, 155.

21 Ibid., pp. 156, 40.

22 Ibid., p. 82.

23 Ibid., p. 145.

24 Ibid., p. 83.

25 Smith, *Realist Thought from Weber to Kissinger*, p. 53.

26 James, *Sovereign Statehood*, p. 129.

27 Ibid., p. 276.

Chapter 4

1 Justin Rosenberg, *The Empire of Civil Society* (London; Verso, 1994), pp. 4–5. Smith points out that in Morgenthau's *Politics among Nations* – that most classic of realist texts – illustrations of statist behaviour are taken from every period of history, and these illustrations have remained intact through each of the book's six editions. M.J. Smith, *Realist Thought from Weber to Kissinger* (London: Louisiana State University Press, 1986), p. 141.

2 Rosenberg, *Empire of Civil Society*, pp. 120–3.

3 Ibid., p. 87. The modern state is basically liberal in character. Onuf agrees: Nicholas Onuf, 'Sovereignty: Outline of a Conceptual History', *Alternatives*, 16, 1991, p. 426.

4 Rosenberg, *Empire of Civil Society*, p. 18.

5 Ibid., p. 127.

6 Ibid., p. 84. Rosenberg argues that the British state, for example, only became sovereign under the Thatcher government in 1979: Ibid., p. 134.

7 F.H. Hinsley, *Sovereignty* (Cambridge: Cambridge University Press, 1986), pp. 21, 121, 125.

8 Ibid., pp. 26–8; David Held, *Political Theory and the Modern State* (Cambridge: Polity, 1989), p. 217.

9 Andrew Vincent, *Theories of the State* (Oxford: Blackwell, 1987), p. 32.

10 Charles Merriam, *History of the Theory of Sovereignty since Rousseau* (New York: Columbia University Press, 1900), p. 11. The concept of sovereignty can 'be traced back to Aristotle': James Rosenau, 'Sovereignty in a Turbulent World' in Gene Lyons and Michael Mastanduno (eds), *Beyond Westphalia?* (Baltimore, MD and London: Johns Hopkins University Press, 1995), p. 192.

11 Hinsley, *Sovereignty*, pp. 31, 43–4. But see ibid., p. 126. In Crick's view, sovereignty was unknown to the ancient Romans: Bernard Crick, 'Sovereignty' in David Sills (ed.), *International Encyclopedia of the Social Sciences* (New York: Macmillan Free Press, 1968), p. 78.

12 Merriam, *History of the Theory of Sovereignty since Rousseau*, p. 11; Vincent, *Theories of the State*, p. 33. This position is also supported by Preston King, *The Ideology of Order* (London: Allen & Unwin, 1974), p. 73.

13 Hinsley, *Sovereignty*, p. 55.

14 Perry Anderson, *Lineages of the Absolute State* (London: New Left Books, 1974), pp. 15 (emphasis added), 28.

15 Vincent, *Theories of the State*, p. 34; Hinsley, *Sovereignty*, pp. 61, 68–9.

16 Anderson, *Lineages of the Absolute State*, pp. 27–8.

17 Merriam, *History of the Theory of Sovereignty since Rousseau*, p. 12; Hinsley, *Sovereignty*, p. 98. See also Crick, 'Sovereignty', p. 77; Kathleen Jones, *Compassionate Authority* (New York and London: Routledge, 1993), pp. 38–9.

18 Hinsley argues that because Machiavelli favoured a mixture of governmental forms 'in which no power was supreme', he was unable to develop a conception of a body politic 'endowed with sovereign power': Hinsley, *Sovereignty*, pp. 98, 113, 116.

19 Ibid., p. 120.

20 Held, *Political Theory and the Modern State*, p. 217; Julian Franklin, 'Introduction' in Julian Franklin (ed.), *Jean Bodin on Sovereignty* (Cambridge: Cambridge University Press, 1992), p. xxiv.

21 King, *Ideology of Order*, p. 79.

22 Franklin, 'Introduction', p. xxiv. See also King, *The Ideology of Order*, p. 84.

23 Franklin, 'Introduction', p. xxiv. Hinsley therefore oversimplifies when he argues that for Bodin 'sovereignty and mere absolutism were different things': Hinsley, *Sovereignty*, p. 122.

24 Crick, 'Sovereignty', p. 78.

25 Hinsley, *Sovereignty*, pp. 130, 142.

26 King, *Ideology of Order*, p. 98 ; Hinsley, *Sovereignty*, p. 143.

27 Rosenberg, *Empire of Civil Society*, p. 137.

28 Ibid.; Stanley Benn, 'Sovereignty' in Paul Edwards (ed.), *Encyclopedia of Philosophy* (New York: Macmillan Free Press, 1967), p. 502.

29 Rosenberg, *Empire of Civil Society*, pp. 138–9.
30 Hinsley, *Sovereignty*, p. 142. See also Murray Forsyth, 'State' in David Miller *et al.* (eds), *The Blackwell Encyclopedia of Political Thought* (Oxford: Blackwell, 1987), p. 506; A.P. D'Entreves, *The Notion of the State* (Oxford: Clarendon Press, 1967), p. 23.
31 Bhikhu Parekh, 'When Will the State Wither Away?', *Alternatives*, 15, 1990, pp. 248–9.

Chapter 5

1 David Held, *Political Theory and the Modern State* (Cambridge: Polity, 1989), p. 221; Jean-Jacques Rousseau, *The Social Contract* (Harmondsworth: Penguin, 1968), pp. 51, 70.
2 F.H. Hinsley, *Sovereignty* (Cambridge: Cambridge University Press, 1986), pp. 154–5; Held, *Political Theory and the Modern State*, pp. 223–4.
3 Charles Merriam, *History of the Theory of Sovereignty since Rousseau* (New York: Columbia University Press, 1900), p. 35.
4 Hinsley, *Sovereignty*, pp. 154–5; Merriam, *History of the Theory of Sovereignty*, p. 27.
5 Hinsley, *Sovereignty*, pp. 146–7. See also Quintin Skinner, 'The State' in Terence Ball *et al.* (eds), *Political Innovation and Conceptual Change* (Cambridge: Cambridge University Press, 1989).
6 Hinsley, *Sovereignty*, p. 149.
7 Ibid., p. 174; Joseph Camilleri and Jim Falk, *The End of Sovereignty?* (Aldershot: Edward Elgar, 1992), pp. 19–21; Merriam, *History of the Theory of Sovereignty*, p. 32.
8 Held, *Political Theory and the Modern State*, p. 224.
9 Leo Strauss, *Natural Right and History* (Chicago: University of Chicago Press, 1953), p. 232.
10 Held, *Political Theory and the Modern State*, p. 223; Hinsley, *Sovereignty*, pp. 222 (emphasis added), 157.
11 Camilleri and Falk, *The End of Sovereignty?*, p. 22; Merriam, *History of the Theory of Sovereignty*, p. 63; Hinsley, *Sovereignty*, p. 156.
12 Francis Coker, 'Sovereignty' in Edward Seligman (ed.), *Encyclopedia of Social Sciences* (New York: Macmillan, 1934), p. 268.
13 Hinsley, *Sovereignty*, p. 223.
14 Preston King, *The Ideology of Order* (London: Allen & Unwin, 1974), pp. 162, 200; Thomas Hobbes, *Leviathan* (Harmondsworth: Penguin, 1968), pp. 113, 189, 192, 199.
15 Rousseau, *Social Contract*, pp. 52, 64; Hoffman, *Beyond the State* (Cambridge: Polity, 1995), pp. 110–11.
16 A.P. D'Entreves, *The Notion of the State* (Oxford: Clarendon Press, 1967), p. 34; Rodney Barker, *Political Legitimacy and the State* (Oxford: Clarendon Press, 1990), pp. 113–16.

17 David Beetham, *The Legitimation of Power* (Basingstoke: Macmillan, 1991), p. 31. See also Hoffman, *Beyond the State*, pp. 81–3.

18 Beetham, *Legitimation of Power*, pp. 138–9.

19 The force which Rousseau sees as destructive of morality and of right, lies nevertheless at the heart of his (impossible) attempt to legitimate the state. Rousseau, *The Social Contract*, pp. 60, 134.

20 Bernard Crick, 'Sovereignty' in David Sills (ed.), *International Encyclopedia of the Social Sciences* (New York: Macmillan Free Press, 1968), p. 81; Bernard Crick, *In Defence of Politics*, 2nd edn (Harmondsworth: Penguin, 1982), pp. 28, 30.

21 Crick, *In Defence of Politics*, pp. 30, 33. See also John Hoffman, *State, Power and Democracy* (Brighton: Wheatsheaf, 1988), p. 37.

22 King, *Ideology of Order*, p. 156.

23 David Easton, 'Political Anthropology' in B.J. Siegel (ed.), *Biennial Review of Anthropology* (Stanford, CA: Stanford University Press, 1959), p. 218; Adrian Leftwich, *Redefining Politics* (London and New York: Methuen, 1983), p. 28.

24 Hinsley, *Sovereignty*, pp. 17, 7; Hobbes, *Leviathan*, p. 227.

25 Hinsley, *Sovereignty*, p. 8; Pierre Clastres, *Society against the State* (New York: Urizen, 1977), pp. 131, 175. Buzan's reference to the state 'understood as tribe' can only be regarded as eccentric: Barry Buzan, 'The Timeless Wisdom of Realism?' in Steve Smith, Ken Booth and Marysia Zalewski (eds), *International Theory: Positivism and Beyond* (Cambridge: Cambridge University Press, 1996), p. 50.

26 Hinsley, *Sovereignty*, p. 8; Lucy Mair, *Primitive Government* (Harmondsworth: Penguin, 1962), p. 12.

27 Simon Roberts, *Order and Dispute* (Harmondsworth: Penguin, 1979), p. 88; Clastres, *Society against the State*, pp. 31, 162, 132; Hedley Bull, *The Anarchical Society* (Basingstoke: Macmillan, 1977), p. 132; Peter Nicholson, 'Politics and Force' in Adrian Leftwich (ed.), *What Is Politics?* (Oxford: Blackwell, 1984), pp. 42–3.

28 Stanley Johnson, *Realising the Public World Order*, Occasional Paper 2 (University of Leicester: Centre for the Study of Public Order, 1993).

29 Hinsley, *Sovereignty*, p. 16; Hoffman, *Beyond the State*, p. 40; Roberts, *Order and Dispute*, pp. 20, 26, 137.

30 Easton, 'Political Anthropology', p. 217.

31 I have argued this case in more detail in *Beyond the State*, p. 88; and *State, Power and Democracy*, pp. 121–2.

32 Hinsley, *Sovereignty*, pp. 16–17.

Chapter 6

1 Joseph Camilleri and Jim Falk, *The End of Sovereignty?* (Aldershot: Edward Elgar, 1992), pp. 33–4; W.J. Stankiewicz, 'Introduction' in W.J.

Stankiewicz (ed.), *In Defense of Sovereignty* (London and Toronto: Oxford University Press, 1969), p. 8; Jacques Maritain, 'The Concept of Sovereignty' in Stankiewicz, *In Defense of Sovereignty*, pp. 43, 50, 56, 64.

2 Maritain, 'The Concept of Sovereignty', pp. 54, 63, 55.

3 Stankiewicz, 'Introduction', p. 8. See also John Hoffman, *State, Power and Democracy* (Brighton: Wheatsheaf, 1988), pp. 148–9.

4 Stankiewicz, 'Introduction', pp. 3, 8, 6.

5 Ibid., p. 8; Plato, *The Republic* (Harmondsworth: Penguin, 1955), p. 336.

6 Aristotle, *The Politics* (Harmondsworth: Penguin, 1962), p. 28. Stankiewicz cites the words of Aristotle as a motto for his introduction. See also Hoffman, *State, Power and Democracy*, pp. 143–9.

7 Harold Laski, *Studies in the Problem of Sovereignty* (New Haven, CT: Yale University Press, 1917), p. 267; Robert Dahl, *Who Governs?* (New Haven, CT and London: Yale University Press, 1961); Alexis de Tocqueville, *Democracy in America* (London and Glasgow: Fontana, 1966), p. 17. See also Bernard Crick, *In Defence of Politics*, 2nd edn (Harmondsworth: Penguin, 1982), p. 67.

8 Harold Laski, *The State in Theory and Practice* (London: George Allen & Unwin, 1935), pp. 21, 24, 27; Bernard Crick, 'Sovereignty' in David Sills (ed.), *International Encyclopedia of the Social Sciences* (New York: Macmillan Free Press, 1968), p. 78.

9 Preston King, *The Ideology of Order* (London: Allen & Unwin, 1974), p. 34.

10 Camilleri and Falk, *The End of Sovereignty?*, p. 203.

11 Daniel Deudney, 'Binding Sovereigns: Authorities and Structures and Geopolitics in Philadelphian Systems' in Thomas J. Biersteker and Cynthia Weber (eds), *State Sovereignty as Social Construct* (Cambridge: Cambridge University Press), pp. 191, 195, 197.

12 Ibid., pp. 204–5, 197.

13 Ibid., pp. 209, 202.

14 Ibid., p. 211, 205–6.

15 Hoffman, *State, Power and Democracy*, p. 152; Deudney, 'Binding Sovereigns', p. 206.

16 Tocqueville, *Democracy in America*, pp. 8, 294, 828.

17 Hoffman, *State, Power and Democracy*, pp. 137–8.

18 Tocqueville, *Democracy in America*, pp. 391–421.

19 Robert Dahl, *Democracy and Its Critics* (New Haven, CT: Yale University Press, 1989), pp. 37, 51, 90.

20 Crick, *In Defence of Politics*, pp. 61–2.

21 Chantal Mouffe, 'Radical Democracy or Liberal Democracy?' in David Trend (ed.), *Radical Democracy* (New York and London: Routledge, 1996), pp. 25, 21–2.

22 Ibid., p. 23. See also Murray Forsyth, 'Carl Schmitt: *The Conception of the Political*' in Murray Forsyth and Maurice Keens-Soper (eds), *The*

Political Classics: Green to Dworkin (Oxford: Oxford University Press, 1996). Darinda Outram comments that Schmitt sees sovereign individuals as 'a positive threat which the state must ward off': Darinda Outram, *The Body and the French Revolution* (New Haven, CT: Yale University Press, 1989), p. 14. My thanks to Laura Brace for drawing this reference to my attention.

23 Mouffe, 'Radical Democracy or Liberal Democracy?', p. 25; Forsyth, 'Carl Schmitt: *The Conception of the Political*', p. 95.

24 Mouffe, 'Radical Democracy or Liberal Democracy?', p. 25.

25 David Held, *Democracy and the Global Order* (Cambridge: Polity, 1995), p. 21.

26 John Hoffman, *Beyond the State* (Cambridge: Polity, 1995), pp. 211–13; see David Held, 'Democracy: From City States to a Cosmopolitan Order' in David Held (ed.), *Prospects for Democracy* (Oxford: Blackwell, 1992), pp. 10–39.

27 Held, *Democracy and the Global Order*, pp. 22, 99–100, 135.

28 Ibid., pp. 233–4.

29 Ibid., p. 233.

30 Ibid., pp. 271, 279.

31 Ibid., pp. 187, 198.

32 Ibid., p. 222.

33 Ibid., p. 208.

34 Ibid., pp. 210, 286.

35 Ibid., p. 191.

Chapter 7

1 Karen Offen, 'Defining Feminism: a Comparative Historical Approach' in Gisela Bock and Susan James (eds), *Beyond Equality and Difference* (London and New York: Routledge, 1992), pp. 74, 70; Maggie Humm, 'Preface' in Maggie Humm (ed.), *Feminisms* (Hemel Hempstead: Harvester Wheatsheaf, 1992), p. xi. Nancy Hirshmann and Christine Di Stefano support Seyla Benhabib's definition of feminism as 'the theoretical articulation of the emancipatory aspirations of women'. Feminists differ about the best way of defining 'emancipation', or indeed 'women', but agree to disagree about terms which 'bring them together as feminists'. Nancy Hirshmann and Christine Di Stefano, 'Introduction: Revision, Reconstruction and the Challenge of the New' in Nancy Hirshmann and Christine Di Stefano (eds), *Revisioning the Political* (Oxford: Westview, 1996), p. 22.

2 Diana Coole, *Women in Political Theory* (Hemel Hempstead: Harvester Wheatsheaf, 1988), pp. 120–3, 144; Moira Gatens, '"The Oppressed State of My Sex": Wollstonecraft on Reason, Feeling and

Equality', in Mary Shanley and Carole Pateman (eds), *Feminist Interpretations and Political Theory* (Cambridge: Polity, 1991); Valerie Bryson, *Feminist Political Theory* (Basingstoke: Macmillan, 1992), pp. 22–7, 55–63; Zillah Eisenstein, *The Radical Future of Liberal Feminism* (London: Longman, 1981), p. 4. See also John Hoffman, *Beyond the State* (Cambridge: Polity, 1995), pp. 148–9.

3 Hoffman, *Beyond the State*, pp. 149–52. See Moira Gatens, 'Power, Bodies and Difference' in Michèle Barrett and Anne Phillips, *Destabilizing Theory* (Cambridge: Polity, 1992), pp. 121–2.

4 Sandra Harding, *The Science Question in Feminism* (New York: Cornell University Press, 1986); Robert Keohane, 'International Relations Theory: Contributions of a Feminist Standpoint' in Rebecca Grant and Kathleen Newland (eds), *Gender and International Relations* (Buckingham: Open University Press, 1991), pp. 41–50; Christine Sylvester, *Feminist Theory and International Relations in a Postmodern Era* (Cambridge: Cambridge University Press, 1994).

5 Nancy Fraser and Linda Nicholson, 'Social Criticism without Philosophy' in Linda Nicholson (ed.), *Feminism/Postmodernism* (London: Routledge, 1990), p. 20; Kathleen Jones, *Compassionate Authority* (New York and London: Routledge, 1993), p. 202. See also Marysia Zalewski, 'Feminist Standpoint Theory Meets International Relations Theory: A Feminist Version of David and Goliath?', *The Fletcher Forum of World Affairs*, 172:2, 1993, p. 15.

6 Jones, *Compassionate Authority*, p. 125; Anna Yeatman, 'A Feminist Theory of Social Differentiation' in Nicholson, *Feminism/Postmodernism*, pp. 292–3.

7 Offen, 'Defining Feminism', p. 83. For an argument that postmodern feminism should be supported over feminist postmodernism, see Sylvester, *Feminist Theory and International Relations*; Nancy Hirshmann, *Rethinking Obligation* (Ithaca, NY: Cornell University Press, 1992).

8 Anna Yeatman, *Postmodern Revisionings of the Political* (New York and London: Routledge, 1994), pp. 6–7. See also Jones, *Compassionate Authority*, p. 182.

9 Heidi Hernes, *Welfare State and Woman Power* (London: Norwegian University Press, 1987), pp. 12–15; Zillah Eisenstein, *The Color of Gender* (Los Angeles: University of California Press, 1994), pp. 34, 172, 219. Contrast this with the earlier argument that the state 'in and of itself institutionalizes patriarchy': Eisenstein, *Radical Future of Liberal Feminism*, p. 227.

10 Judith Allen, 'Does Feminism Need a Theory of the State?' in Sophie Watson (ed.), *Playing the State* (London: Verso, 1990), pp. 22, 27.

11 Catherine MacKinnon, *Toward a Feminist Theory of the State* (London: Harvard University Press, 1989), pp. 161, 169, 238.

12 Allen, 'Does Feminism Need a Theory of the State?', p. 22; Mac-Kinnon, *Toward a Feminist Theory of the State*, pp. 119, 169, 170, 175.

13 Gerda Lerner, *The Creation of Patriarchy* (New York: Oxford University Press, 1986), pp. 76, 89, 101, 106, 212.

14 Hoffman, *Beyond the State*, pp. 153–4; Lerner, *The Creation of Patriarchy*, pp. 42, 46; V. Spike Peterson, 'Security and Sovereign States: What is at Stake in Taking Feminism Seriously' in V. Spike Peterson (ed.), *Gendered States* (Boulder, CO and London: Lynne Rienner, 1992), pp. 38, 33, 45.

15 Allen, 'Does Feminism Need a Theory of the State?', pp. 22, 27, 30.

16 Robert Connell, 'The State, Gender and Sexual Politics: Theory and Appraisal', *Theory and Society*, 19, p. 539.

17 Jones, *Compassionate Authority*, pp. 43, 50, 67, 89–90.

18 Ibid., pp. 107, 117–18.

19 Ibid., pp. 143, 148, 177–9, 153, 214. See also Kathleen Jones, 'What Is Authority's Gender?' in Hirshmann and Di Stefano, *Revisioning the Political*, p. 84.

20 Jones, *Compassionate Authority*, pp. 202, 207.

21 Simone de Beauvoir, *The Second Sex* (Harmondsworth: Penguin, 1972), pp. 18, 29, 125, 96, 135–6, 161, 397, 639.

22 Ibid., p. 726.

23 Ibid., pp. 359, 360.

24 Ibid., pp. 616, 691.

25 Laura Brace, 'Imagining the Boundaries of a Sovereign Self' in Laura Brace and John Hoffman (eds) *Reclaiming Sovereignty* (London: Pinter, 1997), pp. 137, 139, 149.

26 Ibid., pp. 139–41, 142–3, 147–9.

27 Offen, 'Defining Feminism', pp. 76, 78, 85.

28 Brace, 'Imagining the Boundaries of a Sovereign Self', pp. 151–2.

29 Brace, 'Imagining the Boundaries of a Sovereign Self', pp. 151–3; Jennifer Nedelsky, 'Law Boundaries and the Bounded Self', *Representations*, 30, 1990, p. 176.

30 Cynthia Daniels, *At Women's Expense* (Cambridge, MA: Harvard University Press, 1993), pp. 25, 32, 131.

31 Ibid., pp. 5, 131, 138–9.

Chapter 8

1 David Lyon, *Postmodernity* (Buckingham: Open University Press, 1994), pp. 7, 18; Michael Ryan, 'Postmodern Politics', *Theory, Culture and Society*, 5, 1988, p. 559; Marianne Marchand and Jane Parpart, 'Exploding the Canon: An Introduction/Conclusion' in Marianne Marchand and Jane Parpart (eds), *Feminism/Postmodernism/Development* (London and New York: Routledge, 1995), p. 2. See also Linda

Hutcheon, *The Politics of Postmodernism* (London and New York: Routledge, 1989); and John Hoffman, *Beyond the State* (Cambridge: Polity, 1995), p. 236.

2 R.B.J. Walker, *Inside/Outside* (Cambridge: Cambridge University Press, 1993), pp. 188–9.

3 Nancy Fraser and Linda Nicholson, 'Social Criticism without Philosophy' in Linda Nicholson (ed.) *Feminism/Postmodernism* (London: Routledge, 1990), pp. 22–3; Hoffman, *Beyond the State*, pp. 163–5; John Hoffman, 'Postmodernism, the State and Politics' in Jane Dowson and Steven Earnshaw (eds), *Postmodern Subjects/Postmodern Texts* (Amsterdam, Rodpi, 1995), pp. 101–15.

4 Richard Ashley, 'Untying the Sovereign State: A Double Reading of the Anarchy Problematique', *Millennium*, 17:2, 1988, p. 228; Richard Ashley, 'Living on Border Lines: Man, Poststructuralism and War' in James Der Derian and Michael Shapiro (eds), *International/Intertextual Relations* (Lexington, MA: Lexington Books, 1989), p. 261. See also Richard Ashley, 'Imposing International Purpose: Notes on a Problematic on Governance' in Ernst Otto-Czempiel and James Rosenau (eds), *Global Changes and Theoretical Challenges* (Lexington, MA: Lexington Books, 1989), pp. 250–90; and Richard Ashley, 'The Achievements of Post-structuralism' in Steve Smith, Ken Booth and Marysia Zalewski (eds), *International Theory: Positivism and Beyond* (Cambridge: Cambridge University Press, 1996), pp. 240–53.

5 Alec McHoul and Wendy Grace, *A Foucault Primer* (London: UCL Press, 1993), pp. 62–3.

6 Ashley, 'Untying the Sovereign State', pp. 230–2, 250.

7 Ibid., pp. 255, 235, 246; Ashley, 'Living on Border Lines', p. 268.

8 Ashley, 'Untying the Sovereign State', p. 234; Ashley, 'Living on Border Lines', p. 319; Hoffman, *Beyond the State*, p. 166.

9 Ashley, 'Untying the Sovereign State', pp. 240, 245; Hoffman, *Beyond the State*, p. 183; Ashley, 'Living on Border Lines', pp. 268–9.

10 R.B.J. Walker and Saul H. Mendlovitz, 'Interrogating State Sovereignty' in R.B.J. Walker and Saul H. Mendlovitz (eds), *Contending Sovereignties* (Boulder, CO and London: Lynne Rienner, 1990), p. 2; Walker, *Inside/Outside*, p. 14; Ashley, 'Untying the Sovereign State', pp. 242, 253–4.

11 Ashley, 'Untying the Sovereign State', p. 244.

12 Ibid., p. 254.

13 Ibid., pp. 228, 234, 254.

14 Ibid., pp. 248, 250, 261; Ashley, 'Living on Border Lines', pp. 320, 279–82.

15 Hoffman, *Beyond the State*, p. 171.

16 Ashley, 'Untying the Sovereign State', p. 251; Anna Yeatman,

Postmodern Revisionings of the Political (New York and London: Routledge, 1994), pp. viii–ix, 9–10.

17 Yeatman, *Postmodern Revisionings of the Political*, pp. ix; 6–7. Sandra Harding, 'Feminism. Science and Anti-Enlightenment Critiques' in Nicholson, *Feminism/Postmodernism*, p. 100. See also Anna Yeatman, 'A Feminist Theory of Social Differentiation', in Nicholson, *Feminism/Postmodernism*, pp. 292–3.

18 Jens Bartelson, *Genealogy of Sovereignty* (Cambridge: Cambridge University Press, 1995), pp. 245–6, 10.

19 Ashley points to the superiority of the dialogue or heterologue over the monologue. But this argument can only be sustained if we assume that modernism is not just an arbitrary sovereign voice, but provides the conceptual tools – reason, history, the individual – upon which postmodernism builds. See Ashley, 'Living on Border Lines', p. 292; Ashley, 'Untying the Sovereign State', p. 242.

20 Ashley, 'Living on Border Lines', p. 291; Ashley, 'Untying the Sovereign State', pp. 227, 243.

21 Ashley, 'Untying the Sovereign State', p. 248.

22 Bartelson, *Genealogy of Sovereignty*, pp. 88, 151; Hedley Bull, 'Martin Wight and the Theory of International Relations', *British Journal of International Relations*, 2, 1985, p. 112; Hedley Bull, *Anarchical Society* (Basingstoke: Macmillan, 1977), pp. 8, 218, 318.

23 Bull, *Anarchical Society*, pp. 267, 152, 9; Hoffman, *Beyond the State*, p. 184.

24 Bull, *Anarchical Society*, pp. 6, 228, 214, 320.

25 Bartelson, *Genealogy of Sovereignty*, p. 244; R.J. Vincent, 'Order in International Politics' in J.D.B. Miller (ed.), *Order and Violence* (Oxford: Clarendon Press, 1990), p. 43; Murray Forsyth, 'The Classical Theory of International Relations', *Political Studies*, 26:3, 1978, p. 416; Bull, *Anarchical Society*, p. 22.

Chapter 9

1 John Hoffman, *Beyond the State* (Cambridge: Polity, 1995), p. 99.

2 Thomas Hobbes, *Leviathan* (Harmondsworth: Penguin, 1968), p. 229; Leo Strauss, *Natural Right and History* (Chicago: University of Chicago Press, 1953), pp. 171, 175.

3 Bertrand de Jouvenel, *Sovereignty* (Cambridge: Cambridge University Press, 1957), p. 246; Carole Pateman, *The Problem of Political Obligation* (Cambridge: Polity, 1985), p. 37.

4 John Locke, *Two Treatises of Civil Government* (London: Dent, 1924), pp. 116, 120, 157–9; Pateman, *Problem of Political Obligation*, p. 63; Hoffman, *Beyond the State*, p. 103.

5 Strauss, *Natural Right and History*, p. 235; Locke, *Two Treatises*, p. 130.
6 Hoffman, *Beyond the State*, p. 103; Strauss, *Natural Right and History*, p. 247.
7 Strauss, *Natural Right and History*, p. 285; Jean-Jacques Rousseau, *The Social Contract and Discourses* (London: Dent, 1968), pp. 201, 208.
8 Rousseau, *Social Contract*, pp. 60, 97, 69.
9 Ibid., pp. 68, 66. See also Strauss, *Natural Right and History*, p. 285.
10 Rousseau, *Social Contract*, pp. 80, 186.
11 David Hume, *Moral and Political Philosophy* (New York: Hafner, 1970), p. 358. See also Pateman, *Problem of Political Obligation*, p. 33; Strauss, *Natural Right and History*, p. 246.
12 H.L. Hart, 'Austin' in David Sills (ed.), *International Encyclopedia of the Social Sciences* (New York: Macmillan Free Press, 1968), pp. 471–2. See also Hinsley, *Sovereignty* (Cambridge: Cambridge University Press, 1986), p. 157.
13 John Stuart Mill, *On Liberty* (Harmondsworth: Penguin, 1974), pp. 68–9.
14 Ibid., pp. 131, 70, 123.
15 Ibid., pp. 68, 166.
16 Ibid., pp. 172–3.
17 Ibid., p. 173.
18 Hobbes, *Leviathan*, p. 255; Rousseau, *Social Contract*, pp. 55, 79.
19 Anthony Arblaster, *The Rise and Decline of Western Liberalism* (Oxford: Blackwell, 1984), p. 74.
20 Mill, *On Liberty*, pp. 68, 144.
21 Hoffman, *Beyond the State*, pp. 106–10.
22 Peter Marshall, *Demanding the Impossible* (London: Fontana, 1993), p. 291; Hoffman, *Beyond the State*, pp. 113–16, 120; G.P Maximoff, *The Political Philosophy of Bakunin* (New York: The Free Press, 1953), p. 146.
23 Marshall, *Demanding the Impossible*, pp. 12, 16; April Carter, 'Anarchism and Violence' in J.R. Pennock and John Chapman (eds), *Anarchism* (New York: New York University Press, 1978), p. 337.
24 Marshall, *Demanding the Impossible*, pp. 649–50; David Miller, *Anarchism* (London: Dent, 1984), p. 51; Hoffman, *Beyond the State*, p. 127.
25 Lesek Kolakowski is cited in Joseph Femia, *Marxism and Democracy* (Oxford: Oxford University Press, 1993), p. 174.
26 Hoffman, *Beyond the State*, pp. 133–4. See also Karl Marx and Frederick Engels, *Collected Works*, Vol. 5 (London: Lawrence and Wishart, 1976), p. 7.
27 Karl Marx, *A Contribution to the Critique of Political Economy* (London: Lawrence and Wishart, 1971), p. 20; Marx and Engels, *Collected Works*, Vol. 5, p. 42. See also Marx and Engels, *Collected Works*, Vol. 4, pp. 197–8.

28 Christine Di Stefano, 'Masculine Marx' in Mary Shanley and Carole Pateman (eds), *Feminist Interpretations and Political Theory* (Cambridge: Polity, 1991), p. 154.

29 Diana Coole, *Women in Political Theory* (Hemel Hempstead: Harvester Wheatsheaf, 1988), p. 200; Valerie Bryson, *Feminist Political Theory* (Basingstoke: Macmillan, 1992), pp. 94–5; Isaac Balbus, *Marxism and Domination* (Princeton, NJ: Princeton University Press, 1982), pp. 268–72; Di Stefano, 'Masculine Marx', p. 154; Hoffman, *Beyond the State*, p. 151.

30 Di Stefano, 'Masculine Marx', p. 142; Norman Geras, 'Democracy and the Ends of Marxism' in Geraint Parry and Michael Moran (eds), *Democracy and Democratization* (London: Routledge, 1994), p. 80; Hoffman, *Beyond the State*, p. 142; John Hoffman, 'Antonio Gramsci: *The Prison Notebooks*' in Murray Forsyth and Maurice Keens-Soper (eds), *Political Classics: Green to Dworkin* (Oxford: Oxford University Press, 1996), p. 75.

31 See R.L. Berki, 'On Marxian Thought and the Problem of International Relations', *World Politics*, 24:1, 1971, pp. 80–105.

Chapter 10

1 Jens Bartelson, *Genealogy of Sovereignty* (Cambridge: Cambridge University Press, 1995), p. 48.

2 Hedley Bull, *Anarchical Society* (Basingstoke: Macmillan, 1977), p. 292. See also Hedley Bull, 'The State's Positive Role in World Affairs', *Daedalus*, 108, 1981, p. 120.

3 Naeem Inayatullah and David Blaney, 'Realizing Sovereignty', *Review of International Studies*, 21:3, 1995, pp. 3–4. See also Marc Williams, 'Rethinking Sovereignty' in Eleonore Kofman and Gillian Youngs (eds), *Globalization* (London: Pinter, 1996), p. 120.

4 Gidon Gottlieb, 'Nations without States', *Foreign Affairs*, May–June 1994, pp. 108, 101. This draws upon the argument in his *Nation against State* (New York: Council on Foreign Relations, 1993).

5 Samuel Barkin and Bruce Cronin, 'The State and the Nation: Changing Norms and the Rules of Sovereignty in International Relations', *International Organization*, 48:1, 1994, pp. 128, 108, 113.

6 Ibid., p. 130.

7 Robert Jackson, *Quasi States, International Relations and the Third World* (Cambridge: Cambridge University Press, 1990), p. 23. See also Inayatullah and Blaney, 'Realizing Sovereignty', p. 16.

8 Justin Rosenberg, *The Empire of Civil Society* (London: Verso, 1994), p. 89.

9 Alan James, *Sovereign Statehood* (London: Allen & Unwin, 1986), p. 48.

10 Jackson, *Quasi States*, p. 182; Larry Siedentop, 'Political Theory and Ideology: The Case of the State' in David Miller and Larry Siedentop (eds) *The Nature of Political Theory* (Oxford: Clarendon, 1983), pp. 73, 61. Nancy Hirshmann argues that we are 'individuals' only in so far as 'we are in relationship': Nancy Hirshmann, 'Revisioning Freedom: Relationship, Context and the Politics of Empowerment' in Nancy Hirshmann and Christine Di Stefano (eds), *Revisioning the Political* (Oxford: Westview, 1996), p. 64.

11 Anna Yeatman, *Postmodern Revisionings of the Political* (New York and London: Routledge, 1994), p. 90.

12 Patricia Mische, 'Ecological Security and the Need to Reconceptualize Sovereignty', *Alternatives*, 14, pp. 390–1.

13 Ibid., pp. 392–3. Ulrich Beck argues that today the word 'risk' denotes 'the threat of destruction of all life on Earth': Ulrich Beck, *Risk Society* (London: Sage, 1992), p. 21.

14 Mische, 'Ecological Security', pp. 396, 392.

15 Ibid., p. 397.

16 Ibid., pp. 396, 398.

17 Robert Garner, 'Ecology and Animal Rights: Is Sovereignty Anthropocentric?' in Laura Brace and John Hoffman (eds), *Reclaiming Sovereignty* (London: Pinter, 1997), pp. 181, 191.

18 Mische, 'Ecological Security', p. 397.

19 Jackson, *Quasi States*, pp. 21–2, 38.

20 Mark Hoffman, 'Agency, Identity and Intervention' in Ian Forbes and Mark Hoffman (eds), *Political Theory, International Relations and the Ethics of Intervention* (Basingstoke: Macmillan, 1993), p. 198.

21 Richard Falk, 'Evasions of Sovereignty' in R.B.J. Walker and Saul H. Mendlovitz (eds), *Contending Sovereignties* (Boulder, CO and London: Lynne Rienner, 1990), p. 76. See also Paul Hirst and Graeme Thompson, *Globalization in Question* (Cambridge: Polity, 1996), p. 171; Mark Zacher, 'The Decaying Pillars of the Westphalian Temple: Implications for International Order and Governance' in James Rosenau and Ernst-Otto Czempiel (eds), *Governance without Government: Order and Change in World Politics* (Cambridge: Cambridge University Press, 1992), p. 100.

22 Inayatullah and Blaney, 'Realizing Sovereignty', p. 17.

23 Ibid., p. 20.

24 C.B. Macpherson, *The Political Theory of Possessive Individualism* (Oxford: Oxford University Press, 1962), pp. 262, 75. See also John Hoffman, *Beyond the State* (Cambridge: Polity, 1995), p. 190.

25 Mische, 'Ecological Security', pp. 414, 411. Neil McCormick argues that the development of the principle of subsidiarity in the EU requires 'a conception of statehood or polity stripped of the old assumptions about

sovereignty': Neil McCormick, 'Liberalism, Nationalism and the Post-sovereign State', *Political Studies*, 44:3, 1996, p. 567. The point is a good one even if the terminology is confused!

26 Mill, *On Liberty*, p. 187. Paul Hirst, 'Is Globalisation a Threat to the Nation State? Ten Key Questions and Some Unexpected Answers', paper presented to The Sovereignty Seminar, Department of Politics and Sociology, Birbeck College, University of London, p. 25, 19 February 1997.

27 Hinsley, *Sovereignty*, pp. 1–2.

Index